Library of
Davidson College

ANCIENT PHILOSOPHY

*Editions
Commentaries
Critical Works*

Edited by
LEONARDO TARÁN
Columbia University

A Garland Series

THOMAS H. BILLINGS

THE PLATONISM OF PHILO JUDAEUS

GARLAND PUBLISHING, INC.
NEW YORK & LONDON
1979

*For a complete list of the titles in this series,
see the final pages of this volume.*

The volumes in this series are printed on acid-free,
250-year-life paper.

Bibliographical note:
This facsimile has been made from a copy in
the Yale University Library (K8.P53.2919b).

Library of Congress Cataloging in Publication Data

Billings, Thomas Henry, 1881–
  The Platonism of Philo Judaeus.

  (Ancient philosophy ; 3)
  Reprint of the author's thesis presented to the
University of Chicago, 1915, and published by University of Chicago Press, Chicago, in 1919.
  Includes bibliographical references and index.
  1. Philo Judæus.   2. Plato—Influence.
        I. Title. II. Series.
  B689.Z7B5   1979   181'.3   78-66560
        ISBN 0-8240-9608-8

Printed in the United States of America

The University of Chicago

THE PLATONISM OF PHILO JUDAEUS

A DISSERTATION
SUBMITTED TO THE FACULTY
OF THE GRADUATE SCHOOL OF ARTS AND LITERATURE
IN CANDIDACY FOR THE DEGREE OF
DOCTOR OF PHILOSOPHY

DEPARTMENT OF GREEK

BY
THOMAS HENRY BILLINGS

THE UNIVERSITY OF CHICAGO PRESS
CHICAGO, ILLINOIS
1919

COPYRIGHT 1919 BY
THE UNIVERSITY OF CHICAGO

All Rights Reserved

Published November 1919

Composed and Printed By
The University of Chicago Press
Chicago, Illinois, U.S.A.

PREFACE

The appearance of another dissertation on a topic connected with Philo seems to need explanation, and, though I have made this explanation at length in the first chapter, it should perhaps be mentioned here. Recent scholarship, while throwing light on the influence of modes of thought that belong to the Hellenistic period, has tended in the case of Philo to obscure the more fundamental character of the influence of Plato. It has seemed necessary to restate the nature and extent of this influence in order to clarify present-day thinking on the content and the influence of Philo's work. The subject was suggested to me by Professor Paul Shorey, of the University of Chicago. I have been directed to fruitful lines of investigation and saved from many errors by Professor Shorey's generous use of his time in reading and discussing the manuscript. Throughout the work I have had the advantage of Dr. Grace Hadley Billings' intimate knowledge of Plato. My indebtedness to printed sources has for the most part been acknowledged in the footnotes. I find, however, that neither in the text nor in the notes have I made plain the extent of my debt to Professor Bréhier. I have had his works on Philo constantly at hand, and, though there are many points of interpretation on which I find myself in disagreement with him, I am deeply indebted, as all students of Philo must be, to his wide and accurate learning and to the admirable lucidity of his method.

THOMAS H. BILLINGS

NORTHFIELD, MINNESOTA
September, 1919

CONTENTS

CHAPTER PAGE
I. INTRODUCTION: A SURVEY OF THE HISTORY OF PHILONIC INTERPRETATION 1
1. Philo as a Christian Father—2. The Trinitarian controversy—3. The period of free investigation—Summary of present-day opinions—Attitude of this treatise.

II. PHILO'S CONCEPTION OF THE ULTIMATE REALITY 13
God and matter—Inconsistencies charged to Philo in his opinions on God—His teaching compared with that of Plato—Comparison of Philo's vocabulary with that of Plato—God as Father—Philô's doctrine of matter compared with that of Plato.

III. THE INTERMEDIARY POWERS 26
Eclecticism of style—Various meanings of the term λόγος—Meaning of the Logos and the Logoi—History of the doctrine of the Logos; Heraclitus; Plato; Aristotle; the Stoics; Philo—Affinities of Philo's Logos with the Platonic Idea of Good—The mythology of the Logos—Platonic sources of this mythology—Sources other than Plato—Philo's indifference to consistency in his mythology.

IV. MAN'S SOUL AND ITS POWERS 47
Philo's ethical interest—The rational and the irrational soul—Teaching of Plato, Aristotle, the Stoics, and Philo on the divisions of the soul—Philo's teaching on the nature of the soul; consideration of expressions which seem to imply materialism—The place of the soul in the composite earthly being—Sensation in Plato, Aristotle, the Stoics, and Philo—The physiology of sensation in Plato and in Philo—Philo's doctrine of divine inspiration and its Platonic parallels—Sensation and the will in Philo and in Plato.

V. ETHICS 72
Philo's doctrine of the ethical aim—Platonic sources of Philo's doctrine—Alleged differences between Philo and Plato in regard to the ideal world and the ethical aim—Alleged confusion of Stoic and Peripatetic doctrines in Philo's teaching—Political virtue—Pleasure—The three ways of attaining virtue—αὐτομαθὴς σοφία—Self-discipline and its aids, love and conscience—Instruction, intellectual and moral—Conclusion.

CHAPTER	PAGE
VI. THE INFLUENCE OF PLATO ON THE PHRASEOLOGY OF PHILO	88

Platonic terminology a part of Philo's mind—1. The figure of the chariot of the soul—2. The figure of the contest—3. The figure of the health and disease of the soul—4. The figure of the bodyguards—5. The figure of the pregnant mind—6. Figures representing the senses and the passions—7. Phraseology suggesting the Platonic ideas—8. Other Platonic figures—9. Philo's use of other striking Platonic passages.

INDEX 105

CHAPTER I

A SURVEY OF THE HISTORY OF PHILONIC INTERPRETATION

The history of Philonic interpretation may be divided into three main periods: first, the period lasting to the middle of the sixteenth century, during which Philo was regarded as a Christian Father; second, the period during which the attitude of scholars on the question of his relation to Plato was determined by their presuppositions in regard to the doctrine of the Trinity; third, the period of free, untrammeled investigation.[1]

1. PHILO AS A CHRISTIAN FATHER

The preservation of so large a body of Philo's works is due to the tradition that originates, so far as we can tell, with Eusebius, the church historian of the fourth century. Struck with the resemblance to the Christian communities of the monastic groups described by Philo in his treatise, "On the Contemplative Life," Eusebius maintains[2] that these are really Christian. He says that there is a tradition that Philo made a journey to Rome during the reign of the Emperor Claudius; that there he met Peter, who was preaching to the Romans at the time, and became a Christian. But it is not only in connection with the monastic communities that Eusebius recognized Christian teaching in Philo. He regarded him as teaching the Christian doctrine of the Trinity.[3] The tradition that Philo was a Christian, once established, is repeated by the later writers on Philo. Jerome[4] goes so far as to include him in the list of Church Fathers. It was not until Dionysius Petavius

---

[1] The history of Philonic interpretation is dealt with by Fabricius, *Bibliotheca Graeca* (1785), IV, 723; Mosheim, note in his translation of Cudworth's *Intellectual System*, pp. 320 ff. in Vol. II of Harrison's translation. See also the résumé of the scholarship of the nineteenth century in Cohn, "Latest Researches on Philo of Alexandria," *Jewish Quarterly Review*, V (1892–93), 24 ff. The ancient *Testimonia* are collected in Vol. I of the Cohn-Wendland edition of Philo, pp. lxxxv–cxiii.

[2] *Hist. Eccl.* ii. 17. 1; p. lxxxix in Cohn-Wendland (hereafter referred to as C.-W.), Vol. I.

[3] *Praep. Evangel.* 7. 13.

[4] *De Viris Illustribus*, chap. 11, "a nobis inter scriptores ecclesiasticos ponitur."

published his great work on doctrine in 1644 that this tradition was definitely challenged.[1]

But while the Church Fathers to the middle of the sixteenth century regarded Philo as a Christian, they still thought of him as a Greek philosopher and almost uniformly connected him with Plato. Clement of Alexandria, it is true, calls him "Philo the Pythagorean,"[2] but Eusebius, writing about a century later, speaks of him as "especially devoted to the philosophical system based on the teachings of Plato and Pythagoras."[3] By the time of Jerome, it had become a fixed tradition to regard Philo as a Platonist. Jerome, in his account of Philo in the *De Viris Illustribus*, chapter 11, quotes a proverb "current among the Greeks," a proverb which, in its Greek form, has served as a basis for much of the discussion on Philo since Jerome's day, ἢ Φίλων πλατωνίζει ἢ Πλάτων φιλωνίζει, "if Philo is not a Platonist, then Plato is a Philonist." The discussions on Philo for many centuries were colored by this striking epigram. Scholars approached the study of his works prepared to connect him in some way with Plato.

But it is surprising to find among those who accept the same formula so wide a variety of opinion as these scholars exhibit. All accept the epigram as containing something permanently true; but some think that it means a likeness in style only;[4] others that the likeness is in thought alone;[5] others accept the proverb at its fullest possible value and find resemblances in both thought and style;[6] still others reduce the proverb to its minimum of meaning and think it means only that Philo is a great philosopher, a second Plato.[7] In the discussions earlier than

[1] For a complete account of the history of this tradition see Conybeare, *Philo about the Contemplative Life*, Oxford, 1895, pp. 321 ff. The tradition was rejected by the scholars of the Reformation but is still accepted by many of the Roman Catholics out of reverence for the authority of Eusebius. Suidas and Photius introduce their accounts of the Eusebian tradition by φασί and λέγουσι.

[2] *Strom.* ii. 482, P.; C.-W., *Testimonia*, I, lxxxxvi.

[3] *Hist. Eccl.* ii. 4. 3; C.-W., *Testimonia*, I, lxxxxviii.

[4] So Augustine *Contra Faustum* xii. 39 (C.-W., I, cv); Isidore of Pelusium, Book 3, Ep. 81, in C.-W., I, cviii.

[5] Theodorus Metochita, *Miscell.*, chap. 16, in C.-W., I, cxi f.

[6] Suidas, s.v. "Φίλων," C.-W., I, cx.

[7] So apparently Photius *Bibl.* Cod. 105 in C.-W., I, cx. The proverb, he says, was due to the admiration with which Philo's power in discourse (λόγοι) inspired "the Hellenists" (τοῖς Ἑλληνισταῖς). "The Hellenists," as Dionysius Petavius points out ("De Trinitate" 1:2, in *De theol. dogm.* ii. 6, edition of 1644), should mean the Hellenistic Jews. The phrase may, however, be Photius' interpretation of Jerome's "apud Graecos." Sophronius' Greek version of Jerome gives Ἑλληνικῶν for Graecos. See C.-W., *Testimonia*, I, ciii.

the thirteenth century, there is little of value. Eusebius, Augustine, Photius, Suidas, Isidore of Pelusium and the others give, each of them, a dogmatic statement of a personal opinion with no attempt at a scientific demonstration. The first attempt at any scientific estimate of Philo's relation to Plato occurs, so far as I can find, in the works of Theodore the Metochite,[1] a Byzantine writer of the thirteenth century.[2] He still feels bound to accept the authority of the proverb quoted by Jerome, and he discusses at some length the various interpretations. His conclusion is that the proverb must mean that Philo is a genuine Platonist. He has rather a poor opinion of Philo's ability and thinks it is absurd to regard the proverb as meaning that Philo was a second Plato. It points, he thinks, to a genuine resemblance between the two thinkers. Like Plato, Philo is interested in the things of the mind, in ethics, and in speculations concerned with numbers. He does not, according to the Metochite, altogether despise natural philosophy, but he is not so much interested in this as in other branches. It is, then, in the direction that his thoughts took, rather than in his ability as a thinker or writer that this interpreter finds the resemblance of Philo to Plato.

Theodore the Metochite is the last scholar whom we need to consider who belongs to the first period of Philonic interpretation. The outstanding feature of this period is the acceptance of Philo as practically a Christian writer. It is interesting to note that throughout this period Philo is neglected by the Jews. On the other hand, his ethical teachings, his interpretations of the Old Testament, his theological doctrines, are freely drawn upon by Christian writers. Justin Martyr probably,[3] Clement of Alexandria certainly,[4] are indebted to him. In the fourth century, Eusebius[5] among the Greeks and Ambrosius[6] among the Latins were especially influenced by him. During this period, Philo's works were drawn upon and large extracts used in the Christian anthologies.[7] His works were translated into Armenian and into Latin so that they were easily accessible to both these branches of the Christian church.

[1] Μετοχίτης — μοναχὸς ἀνήκων εἰς μετόχιον, ἐπώνυμον πολλῶν συγγραφέων. Μετόχιον-μικρὸν κοινοβιακὸν μοναστήριον.
Constantides, *Lex. Magnum Graecum.*

[2] *Miscell.*, chap. 16. See C.-W., I, cxi.

[3] Purves, *The Testimony of Justin Martyr to Early Christianity* (New York, 1888), p. 153, with note 2.

[4] See C.-W., I, lx, and footnotes in the same volume, pp. 172, 226, 236, 241, 242, 272.

[5] *Ibid.*, p. lxi.   [6] *Ibid.*, p. lxii.

[7] For list and description see *ibid.*, pp. lxvii, lxviii.

2. THE TRINITARIAN CONTROVERSY

Up to the middle of the sixteenth century, then, Philo was almost universally venerated by the Christian church. He was traditionally connected with Plato, but no one seems to have thought that Platonism was incompatible with Christianity. The connection of Philo with Plato was so firmly fixed in the minds of scholars that they approached him expecting to be reminded of Plato. When some few freed themselves from this presupposition, they were compelled by the tradition to regard Philo as a great, original thinker whose thoughts were in some sense authoritative. The first mark of the new period we are now to consider is that Philo is criticized and that thinkers do not hesitate to differ from him.

Dionysius Petavius, as I mentioned above, published in 1644 his great work on *Dogma*. It is in this work that we first find any objection raised to Philo's theological opinions. Even Theodore the Metochite thought that these opinions, though not original, were true enough.[1] Dionysius is courageous enough to find fault with Philo's conclusions.[2] He censures Christian writers who, in their zeal to find the truth in all places, have too readily accepted as Christian doctrines which were in reality opposed to the true faith. Turning to an examination of the proverb quoted by Jerome, he says that in style Philo and Plato are utterly unlike. The resemblance between them is in thought rather than in style. The doctrine of the Trinity as taught by Philo is, he says, Platonic, not Christian, in that it includes the doctrine of the subordination of the second person of the Trinity. Plato and Philo he regarded as in agreement, but as not Christian.

The question raised by Dionysius as to Philo's doctrine of the Trinity was the center about which most of the Philonic scholarship of the next century and a half revolved.[3] Petrus Allixius in his *Judicium Ecclesiae Judaicae in Unitarios* reverted to the old Eusebian tradition, supposing, as a later writer says,[4] "that the Socinians and the Jews might be more easily refuted if it could be shown that the most eminent of the Jews, previously to the introduction of Christianity, entertained the same opinions as ourselves on the doctrine of the Trinity." Allixius

---

[1] ἔοικέ γε ὅμως περιττός εἶναί τις τὴν σοφίαν ἀνήρ. *Miscell.*, chap. 16. C.-W., I, cxi.

[2] "De Trinitate," 1:2, in *De theol. dogm.* ii. 7 (edition of 1644).

[3] Summarized by Mosheim, note to Cudworth's *Intellectual System*. See edition by Harrison (1845), II, 320 ff. In what immediately follows I have depended largely on Mosheim and on Fabricius, *Bibliotheca Graeca* (1785), IV, 723.

[4] Mosheim, *op. cit.*, p. 323.

minimized the Platonic influence in Philo and regarded him as belonging to the Eclectic school which, according to Suidas,[1] flourished at Alexandria under Potamon in the time of Augustus. In his zeal to give Philo's views the authority that belongs to the classic period of Greek philosophy, he tried to show that Potamon was an Athenian contemporary of Alexander the Great. This last effort was, of course, absurd, but the suggestion that Philo was an Eclectic was one destined to bear fruit. It is interesting to see that Allixius seems to take it for granted that Platonism and Christianity are two different and incompatible things.

Allixius was answered by Le Clerc,[2] who tried to show that Philo was a Platonist. From this he and those who thought with him inferred that "the three natures of Philo do not differ from Plato's three first principles of things." These three principles they regarded as very similar to the three powers of the Arians.[3] The controversy was waged with great ingenuity and learning. Those who were unable to regard Philo as a Platonist by no means agreed in regarding him as a pre-Christian witness for Christianity. Jonsius[4] maintained that Philo's thought was Jewish pure and simple, with no admixture of Greek philosophy. Lipsius[5] contended that he was a Stoic. A number of writers took up Allixius' suggestion and maintained that he was an Eclectic.[6]

The arguments used during this controversy were seldom such as would carry weight today. There was no careful weighing of the evidence drawn from a first-hand study of the author with the help of philological science. The chief arguments used to refute the theory that Philo was a Platonist will serve to illustrate the type of reasoning. They were (1) that Plato is never quoted by Philo as the founder of his tenets; (2) that Plato's philosophy cannot well be associated with the Jewish religion; (3) that Philo at times refutes Plato. Jonsius' arguments are interesting. He declares that the Philo referred to in the proverb quoted by Jerome must be another Philo and bases this conclusion on the unsupported statement that the works of Philo show no traces of the Platonic spirit. Josephus, he says, when he spoke of Philo as skilled

[1] Suidas, s.v. Ποτάμων 'Αλεξανδρεύs. Gaisford (Oxford, 1834), p. 3058.

[2] See in Mosheim and Fabricius, loc. cit.

[3] Mosheim, op. cit., pp. 323 f.

[4] "De Script. Hist. Phil.," Book 3, chap. 4, p. 14, in Fabricius, De Platonismo Phil. Jud. in Opuscula (Hamburg, 1738), p. 154.

[5] See Fabricius, Bibl. Graeca (1785), IV, 724, col. 1, in note (h) to p. 723.

[6] See for example, the preface to the Geneva edition of 1613 and others referred to by Fabricius, Bibl. Graeca (1785), IV, 723.

in philosophy, meant by philosophy just the religious teachings of the Jews. This statement too is quite unsupported.

But while the scholars of this period were given to making unsupported statements in order to bolster up some theological position, the advance they made in Philonic interpretation was of great importance. The superstition of Philo's adherence to Christianity was finally discarded and the traditional linking of his name with that of Plato had now to take its place alongside of other competing theories and be tested on its merits. It still had first claim to consideration because it had remained so long undisputed, but its claims to exclusive attention were definitely set aside.

3. THE PERIOD OF FREE INVESTIGATION

The last period, that of free, disinterested investigation, began with the publication in 1693 of Fabricius' dissertation *De Platonismo Philonis Judaei*.[1] The traditional theory that Platonism gives us the clue to Philo's thought is supported in this treatise by a scholarly investigation of the traces of Platonic doctrines that are found in his writings. The position taken by Fabricius brought Philo into great favor during the eighteenth century. As a follower of Plato, he shared in the glory of his master and was regarded with great respect by the Cambridge Platonists, Henry More, Smith, and Cudworth.[2] These thinkers had a world-wide influence and drew scholars to a fresh study of the masters in whom they professed to find their inspiration.

The most interesting of the studies of Philo produced under this fresh stimulus is that of Mosheim, a German scholar, who in 1773 issued a Latin translation of Cudworth's *Intellectual System* with copious notes of his own. One of these notes[3] is a complete study of Philo Judaeus, brief but clear, definite, and with arguments supported by a wide and accurate knowledge of Philo's works. The conclusions drawn are in some respects new. The author thinks that Philo had not sufficient powers of intellect to discover for himself the philosophy we find in his writings and that this philosophy must have been current at Alexandria "either universally or among the Jews." The principle of interpretation which Mosheim adopts is that Philo's meaning in any particular passage should be estimated by the standard of those pas-

---

[1] *Opuscula* (Hamburg, 1738), pp. 147–60.

[2] See the article on the Cambridge Platonists in Stewart, *Myths of Plato, ad. fin.*

[3] This note is most accessible to English readers in Harrison's edition of the *Intellectual System*, II, 320 ff.

sages which are less figurative. Interpreters should study Philo's style and mark its redundance in figures and bold metaphors. He also calls attention to the two systems in Philo, the popular religion on the one hand and the more sublime and recondite on the other. Following these principles, Mosheim comes to the conclusion that Philo followed a philosophy current in Alexandria in his day; that this philosophy agreed in large part with that of Plato, but had a certain admixture of other teachings, drawn perhaps from Oriental sources, teachings which cannot be found, explicitly at least, in the writings of Plato. Philo was not, however, he thinks, completely devoted to this philosophy but took care to accommodate it to the law and religion of the Jews.

These conclusions of Mosheim struck a severe blow at a figure which had for centuries been an idol of the philosophical schools, and since the appearance of Mosheim's work there has been no lack of men ready to decry Philo as an industrious, but rather weak-minded, eclectic. Ritter in his *History of Philosophy* (1836–37)[1] declares that Philo mingles promiscuously doctrines of Plato, the Pythagoreans, the Peripatetics, and Stoics, and that he does so, not so much from any eclectical method, as from a persuasion that he was at perfect liberty to substitute one for the other as it suited his purpose, "he being, by the character of his mind, incapacitated to discern the difference in the points of view from which they severally proceeded."[2] Ritter thinks, however, that in spite of the mixture of heterogeneous elements in Philo, all his statements are based on certain general principles which come from Oriental sources and are religious rather than philosophical.[3]

The lack of coherence which Mosheim, and more especially Ritter, find in Philo's thought, occupies his interpreters at the present day. While there have not been wanting scholars of note during the last century who have upheld Philo's consistency and retained him as one of the great thinkers,[4] there has been a strong current of opinion which has regarded him as of only second-rate power. Zeller[5] thinks that Philo wavers between Stoicism and a Platonism which is fundamentally irreconcilable with it. Heinze[6] finds these and other irreconcilable elements.

[1] The book was translated into English by Morrison and issued at London in 1846. For Philo see Vol. IV, pp. 407–78.

[2] *Op. cit.*, p. 409.   [3] *Op. cit.*, p. 411.

[4] Neander regarded Philo as a consistent Platonist. *History of Dogma* (Ryland: London, 1866), I, 38. See also Drummond, *Philo Judaeus and the Jewish Alexandrian Philosophy*, and among recent books, Bentwich, *Philo*, Philadelphia, 1910; Inge, article "Philo" in Hastings' *Encyclopedia of Religion and Ethics*.

[5] *Phil. der Griech.* iii. 2. 328–418.   [6] *Lehre v. Logos*, Oldenburg, 1872.

One of the most quoted of recent German dissertations in this field[1] regards him as reproducing the doctrines of Posidonius and questions whether he had any first-hand knowledge of Plato. Bréhier,[2] the great French scholar, develops the thesis of Ritter and demonstrates Philo's connection with Egyptian mystery religions, with the Peripatetic, Skeptic, Stoic, and Epicurean schools, in fact with the most widely varying and most utterly irreconcilable doctrines. This school of interpretation is interested in Philo as a sort of storehouse of all the theological ideas of the world of his day. It is interesting to see that Jewish scholars have now taken up Philo and are among his warmest defenders.[3]

It is necessary to consider in detail one tendency in recent scholarship which has had its influence on Philonic interpretation. A considerable group of German scholars have tended to regard Philo as reproducing the doctrines of Posidonius, the Platonizing Stoic who taught at Rhodes. Diels, in his *Doxographi Graeci*, pp. 19 and 201, shows that Posidonius had a great influence on the thought of the subsequent generations. August Schmekel[4] makes Posidonius the source of the opinions held in common by Cicero and Varro, and again, of those held in common by Cicero and Sextus Empiricus. The tendency, begun by Diels and so strongly developed by Schmekel, to make Posidonius the prime source for the thought of the centuries immediately before and after the beginning of our era, was carried still farther by Richard Heinze, who discovers in Posidonius the source of a great part of the myths of Plutarch.[5] If Posidonius had the influence that this group of scholars assign to him, it is unlikely that Philo, living as he did in Alexandria,

[1] M. Apelt, "De rationibus quibusdam quae Philoni Alexandrino cum Posidonio intercedunt," in *Commentationes Jenenses*, VIII, 91–141.

[2] *Les idées philosophiques et religieuses de Philon d'Alexandrie*, Paris, 1908. Arnim, *Quellenstudien zu Philo* (Berlin, 1888) showed Philo's use of the works of the Skeptic Aenesidemus and his dependence on Stoic sources. See Cohn, *Jewish Quarterly Review*, V, 27 f.

[3] See, for example, Montefiore, "Florilegium Philonis," *Jewish Quarterly Review*, VII, 481–545; Horowitz, *Das platonische Νοητὸν Ζῷον und der philonische Κόσμος Νοητός*, Marburg, 1900; Bentwich, *Philo*, Philadelphia, 1910.

[4] *Die Philosophie der mittleren Stoa* (Berlin, 1892), pp. 85 ff. and 132–54.

[5] In "Xenocrates," pp. 125 ff. Maximilian Adler, "Quibus ex fontibus Plutarchus libellum de facie in orbe lunae hauserit," *Dissertationes Vindobonenses*, Vol. X, Part II, p. 161, goes farther than Heinze in assigning to Posidonius the mythical elements in Plutarch. The arguments of these two writers are analysed by Roger Miller Jones in his dissertation on *The Platonism of Plutarch* (Menasha, Wis., 1916), pp. 52–56. Mr. Jones has shown that it is impossible to regard Posidonius as the source.

a center of learning, would escape. Mathilda Apelt in her dissertation *De rationibus quibusdam quae Philoni Alexandrino cum Posidonio intercedunt*[1] traces to Posidonius all the doctrines of Philo which can be grouped under the name of mysticism. All these, she says, can be found in Posidonius either hinted at or distinctly expressed. This conclusion is reached by arguments far from convincing. It is not sufficient proof of the Posidonian origin of a special doctrine to show parallels between, for example, Seneca and Philo and declare that both draw from Posidonius.[2] Miss Apelt's reference to Hirzel's note[3] in this connection is hardly warranted. Hirzel shows that there is a resemblance between Seneca, *Ep.* 88, and the opinions of Posidonius on the question of the value to be assigned to the encyclic studies. Posidonius, he says, was therefore in accord with the other Stoics on this question.[4] Miss Apelt has made an unwarranted use of these moderate statements when she says, with a bare reference to this note of Hirzel, that Seneca's letter "prope tota e Posidonio fluxisse videtur." There is undoubtedly a body of opinion held in common by a considerable group of thinkers who lived during the centuries immediately following Posidonius. We may, as Bevan points out, call this "Posidonius," but there is no sufficient proof for regarding Posidonius as its originator.[5]

The eagerness to discover parallels in Philo to other writers has had the unfortunate effect of serving to intensify the impression of his uncritical eclecticism. In interpreting Philo, it is wrong to begin by searching for such parallels. Philo can be appreciated only when the task to which he set himself is understood. He was educated as a Greek,[6] his mind was stored with the thoughts of Greek philosophy and literature,[7] and his works show that it was on Greek speculations that he nourished his own spiritual and intellectual life. At the same time, he was a loyal Jew with an enthusiastic pride in Jewish monotheism and morality[8] and a loyal acceptance of the Scriptures,[9] the traditions,[10]

[1] *Comm. Phil. Jen.*, Vol. VIII, Part I, pp. 91–141.

[2] *Op. cit.*, pp. 118–19.   [3] *Untersuchung. zu Ciceros Phil. Schrift.*, II, 525, note.

[4] For the Stoic attitude to encyclic studies see Hirzel, *loc. cit.;* Zeller, *Stoics, Epicureans, and Skeptics*, pp. 62–64.

[5] *Stoics and Skeptics* (Oxford, 1913), p. 95.

[6] *De cong. erud.* 74–76.   [7] Siegfried, *Philo v. Alex.*, pp. 31–141.

[8] *Sp. leg.* 2:166; *Sp. leg.* 4:179–82; *V.M.* 1:148–49; *V.M.* 2:211–16; *De Jos.* 42 f.; *De Ab.* 98.

[9] *V.M.* 1:1; *V.M.* 2:12–17, 25, 36; *Mut. nom.* 60–62.

[10] *V.M.* 2:25–36; *V.M.* 1:1–4; *Somn.* 2:123.

and the ceremonies of his ancestral faith. He believed that all the truth of all the schools of Greek thought received full justice in Judaism.[1] His more or less conscious reasoning seems to have been that Plato's thoughts were true, therefore all Plato's thoughts were to be found in the Books of Moses. Now the philosophy of Plato can be found in detail in the Books of Moses only by straining language to the breaking point and beyond.[2] The Greek world was, however, accustomed to just such straining of language. The Stoic philosophers found their own ideas in Homer and the conviction grew that ancient books were allegorical presentations of philosophy.[3] It was no new and unheard-of method that Philo used when he interpreted the Book of Genesis as the story of the progress of the human soul.[4] By regarding the stories of the Book of Genesis as allegory, he gave formal recognition to the authority and supremacy of the law and at the same time secured the freedom to think as his training demanded.

But if the same truth is to be found expressed in such diverse forms as the Platonic dialogues and the Books of the Law, such comparatively slight variations as that between the Stoic and Platonic statements are of no importance whatever. Philo was convinced that there was fundamental agreement. For example, the Platonic ideas, the Stoic Logoi, the Old Testament angels, the Greek demons are the same.[5] This does not necessarily mean that he did not see the varying points of view from which these severally proceeded. Indeed he saw these differences very clearly. He wages a vigorous war against what he calls the atheism and materialism of the Stoic philosophy.[6] But certain ideas and conceptions are, from his point of view, identical in spite of differences in background.

The identification of similar ideas leads to a peculiar eclecticism of style throughout the entire field of Philo's works. Looking at Greek philosophy as he did from a standpoint which he regarded as superior,

[1] *Mig. Ab.* 90–94. Cf. *Sp. leg.* 2:62–64, 163, 165–67. Moses is said in *Quis rer. div.* 214 to have originated the doctrine of Heraclitus.

[2] This does not contradict the contention of Bentwich, *op. cit.*, pp. 171, 172, that Judaism and Platonism are akin.

[3] For a study of the history of the allegorical method of interpretation, see Boissier, *La fin du paganisme*, I, 310; Mrs. Hersman, *Studies in Greek Allegorical Interpretation*, Chicago, 1907.

[4] So Bréhier, introduction to the *Allegories*, Paris, 1909; Massebieau, *Classement des œuvres de Philon* (Paris).

[5] See below, pp. 28 ff., especially p. 28, n. 4. For the type of reasoning see Case, *Evolution of Early Christianity*, p. 183.

[6] See Bentwich, *op. cit.*, pp. 63–65, 95; *Mig. Ab.* 178–81.

he seemed to see that the differences of the schools were in many cases a mere matter of terminology. By varying the expression of his ideas he emphasizes similarities and establishes parallels strongly and closely. No doubt this variation of terminology and phrasing was in part adopted with an apologetic purpose. The leaders of the Dispersion were under the constant necessity of counteracting the attraction of Gentile speculation in order to retain their own people.[1] By his eclecticism in philosophical vocabulary, Philo exhibits Judaism as the transcendent philosophy, which gives place to all that is true in all schools of Greek speculation.

The shifting vocabulary is one of the main sources of difficulty in the interpretation of Philo's thought. The difficulty is increased by the fact that Philo has the same flexibility of spirit that has confused the interpreters of Plato.[2] He sometimes uses the language of religious ecstasy, sometimes that of the philosophical thinker, sometimes that of the mystical poet.[3] But in spite of these variations in terminology and point of view, in spite, too, of the complete absence of system in the presentation, and the constant highly metaphorical character of the style inseparable from the use of the allegorical method of interpretation, the careful student can find underlying presuppositions to which Philo holds throughout and which determine all his thought.

The clue to his thought is to be found in Platonism in its two aspects. There is a basis of clear, logical reasoning with a frank recognition of the limits of human thought. Then, using the principles of speculative idealism, he gives a probable account of the universe—particularly of man and his duties and relations. He is convinced that life comes to its fulfilment, not in pursuit of the lower life of the body, but in the life of the spirit. It scarcely needs to be said that he is no mere copyist of Plato. The intervening centuries had by no means been barren in the fields of philosophy and science. Jewish elements naturally enter into his thought.[4] Again, his interest is primarily religious and theological, and

[1] Hart, "Philo of Alexandria," *Jewish Quarterly Review*, XVII, 79; Bentwich, *op. cit.*, p. 92.

[2] Shorey, *Unity of Plato's Thought*, p. 5.

[3] The Conybeare edition of the *De Vita Contemplativa*, p. 258, gives an interesting example. To adopt or persevere in the Jewish religion is depicted in Philo as (1) a flight from idolatry to serve the one true God; (2) in philosophical language, as an ascent from sense to reason; (3) in the language of ethics, as the victory of reason in the soul; (4) in mystical language, as a transition to the promised land.

[4] For Jewish elements in Philo, see Bentwich, *op. cit.*, pp. 49–52; Ritter, *Philon. u.d. Halacha*, summarised in Cohn, "Latest Researches on Philo of Alexandria," *Jewish Quarterly Review*, V, 32.

this bias determines the emphasis he lays on the different aspects of Plato's thought. Ideas originating in Plato are at times expanded and developed in certain directions with details that come from later sources. The point of view is, however, Platonic. The following chapters will deal with Philo's solution of the more important problems of philosophy and illustrate the influence of Plato's thought and language in those fields. A final chapter will show the influence of Plato over the warp and woof of Philo's style and the way in which Philo's thought in all spheres naturally tended to shape itself in the language of Plato.

CHAPTER II

PHILO'S CONCEPTION OF THE ULTIMATE REALITY

In harmony with Plato and against the Stoics, Philo teaches a dualistic conception of the universe. He believes in a God who brings order and law into the world of flux. But this power that shapes in the physical world the images of His own thought[1] cannot make those images perfect. Matter is always to some extent recalcitrant.[2] Physical necessity limits God's activity and distorts His work. God and matter stand opposed to one another.[3]

The aim of Philo's work was to show that, of these two elements, the spiritual alone has genuine value and that therefore man's life can come to its fulfilment only in the life of the spirit.[4] He is convinced that the sensible world, with its manifold allurements to materialistic endeavor and sense enjoyment, has not the reality that to our perceptions it seems to have.[5] It is subject to change and decay, and nothing in it can give rest to the soul. Such rest comes only from the knowledge of that true reality in which there is no variableness, neither shadow of turning.[6] It is only through the apprehension of this principle of all being that man can himself rise above the constant press of the material and sensual life into that realm of being where virtue is recognized as the only good.[7] It is, then, of supreme importance that men should be made aware of the permanent reality of which the world is but a distorted reflexion. This true reality is the mind or will which is beyond all existence as its cause and principle, the living, self-conscious Being who has made this universe and who now governs and guides it.

---

[1] The thought of God is the archetypal seal of which this world is the impression. *De op. mund.* 25.

[2] Cf. ἀγόμενος ὑπὸ τῆς σωματικῆς ἀνάγκης, *Leg. all.* 2:28 and Plato *Timaeus* 46 DE; 47 E ff. where ἀνάγκη is distinguished from νοῦς.

[3] This will be illustrated throughout the present chapter.

[4] This topic will be dealt with in detail below. For the present see *Quaes. in Gen.* 1:6.

[5] *Conf. ling.* 52, 125 f.; *De eb.* 171–74, 186–89.

[6] *Mut. nom.* 175; *Somn.* 1:249; 2:219, 223, 225, 228–32.

[7] *Fug. et Inv.* 22, 193; *Mut. nom.* 34, 209; *Somn.* 2:70. For other passages see below, p. 83, notes 7 and 8.

In his description of this ultimate reality, Philo has been accused of a double inconsistency. On the one hand it is said that while he regards the ultimate reality as an impersonal principle, the supreme genus comprehending in itself all the multiplicity of species, he puts alongside of this the Jewish conception of a living, personal God.[1] Others point out that, while he insists that God absolutely transcends the universe, he is equally insistent on the Stoic doctrine that the universe is created, filled, and governed by Him.[2] These inconsistencies, if such they may be called, are certainly present in Philo's thought, but it cannot be granted that they are due to an imperfect fusion in his mind of the opposing doctrines of Judaism and Hellenism or Stoicism and Platonism. They are already present, fully developed, in Plato. But before the affinities in thought and language between Plato and Philo are illustrated in detail, the nature of these inconsistencies must be further examined.

In the first place, then, Philo thinks of God as the ultimate reality, as the supreme genus, but this does not exclude the notion of personality. We shall have to consider the same problem in connection with the doctrine of the Logos. In *Sophist* 248 E, Plato tells us that being as such cannot be conceived without soul and mind. For every religious man, the ultimate reality must be more than a mere dead, logical principle. Plato tends, under the influence of the religious emotions, to make the ideas into active powers. The principle of all life, the unity transcending the difference of subject and object, maintaining its own identity in all the variety of its manifestations, is very naturally thought of as itself a living will. Once the personality of this supreme idea is granted, the religious imagination represents it as an object of desire, as including in itself all the qualities which we attribute to the perfect soul, among them, self-giving love and fellowship with other souls. The inconsistency is not peculiar to Philo or to Plato.

The second inconsistency, that between the transcendence and the immanence of God, to use a modern expression, is an inconsistency which no system can escape which holds to the doctrine of an unchanging reality behind the world of sense.[3] Exactly the same difficulty presents itself in connection with Plato's theory of ideas. The ideas are at once tran-

---

[1] Bréhier, *Id. phil. et relig.*, pp. 69 ff.

[2] Heinze, *Lehre v. Logos*, pp. 208 ff., especially 210. Cf. Wendland, *Hell. Röm. Kult.*, p. 115.

[3] See Shorey, *Unity of Plato's Thought*, pp. 6, 7, 39; Jowett, "Introduction to the Parmenides," in Jowett's *Plato*, IV, 38–43; Inge, article on "Philo" in Hastings' *Encyclopedia of Religion and Ethics*.

scendent and immanent. Plato can represent the relation between them and the particulars only by a series of metaphors.[1]

In view of such considerations it must not be hastily assumed that Philo is holding two incompatible doctrines if, in spite of his emphasis on the transcendence of God, he frequently uses the language of Stoicism in speaking of His immanence.[2] One expression must here be considered. God, Philo says, fills all things, not with His thought only, but with His essence.[3] This expression seems to imply the complete adoption of the doctrine of the Stoics, with the materialistic conception of the interpenetration of matter.[4] The context shows, however, in every case where it is used, that this expression does no more than emphasize God's omnipresence. His essence is opposed to thought, not because it is matter, but because it is something beyond thought. God is present, not as we in thought participate in events far distant in space or time, but actually present. It is not surprising that Philo has to use metaphors from the material world to express the immanence of the transcendent God. We may compare Plato's use of μετέχειν to represent the relation of the particular to the idea and the criticism of the expression in *Parmenides* 131 A, 132 D.[5]

Another expression used of God which has been similarly interpreted in a Stoic sense is ὁ τῶν ὅλων νοῦς.[6] In *Leg. all.* 1:91, He is said to be ἡ τῶν ὅλων ψυχὴ κατὰ ἔννοιαν. The qualification κατὰ ἔννοιαν is significant in view of the passage in *Mig. Ab.* 181: μήτε γὰρ τὸν κόσμον μήτε τὴν τοῦ κόσμου ψυχὴν τὸν πρῶτον εἶναι θεόν. The apparent contradiction disappears when we see that in *Mig. Ab.* 181 he is speaking of God as He is in His essence, while the other phrases are used to express our thought of Him. In His essence He stands outside the universe. Not He but His powers support it (*Mig. Ab.* 182). By analogy we can speak of Him as the νοῦς of the universe but the analogy is not perfect. Our νοῦς does not create our body. It is in its essence confined and contained by the body. God is beyond the universe not in thought only but in essence and He has created it. (*Mig. Ab.* 192–94). The description of

---

[1] See Shorey, *loc. cit.*   [2] Heinze, *Lehre v. Logos*, p. 209.

[3] *De sac. A. et C.* 67; *Quod det. pot.* 153–55; *De post. C.* 6, 7, 30; *De gig.* 27, 47; *Leg. all.* 3:4.

[4] See Bréhier's note on *Leg. all.* 3:4 in his edition of the *Allegories* and compare *Aet. Plac.* I, 7, 33, Zeller, *Stoics, Epicureans, and Skeptics*, p. 148.

[5] Cf. Shorey, *Unity*, pp. 36 f.

[6] *Mig. Ab.* 186, 192–94; *De gig.* 40 f.; Cf. *Quis rer. div.* 155.

God as the νοῦς τῶν ὅλων, though Stoic,[1] originates with Plato.[2] Philo's thought is here much more akin to Plato's in that the world-soul is distinguished from the πρῶτος θεός. Yet in ordinary speech about God the familiar language of Stoicism is used.

A more detailed study of Philo's doctrine of God shows beyond all question his essential agreement with Plato. It has been objected that God in Plato is the Idea of Good and as such is a part of the ideal world to be grasped by our thought, while in Philo He is beyond the world of ideas and we must pass even beyond mind to receive the vision of Him.[3] This interpretation of Philo is correct, but he is not in this respect to be contrasted with Plato. We cannot baldly identify Plato's God with the Idea of Good,[4] and, whether we make this identification or not, God is still for Plato "beyond the world of ideas." The Idea of Good is ἐπέκεινα τῆς οὐσίας (*Rep.* 509 B) just as, for Philo, God is beyond the world of ideas as their ultimate cause and as the most generic idea.[5] As objective ἀρχή, the Idea of Good in Plato is never attainable in human knowledge.[6] The identification of God with the Idea of Good cannot, however, be maintained as a doctrine of Plato. With much greater plausibility, the God of Plato may be identified with τὸ ὄν. The identification is clearly made in *Sophist* 249 A, where, in an eloquent digression, Plato speaks of being as having soul and mind. Logically, pure being is unknown, according to Plato.[7] It is a religious concept and Plato recognizes that as a logical principle it does not exist.[8]

Since this is so, it cannot be maintained that the ecstasy in which the vision of reality is received is for Plato more intellectual in its character than it is for Philo.[9] The moral preparation which both thinkers deem necessary for the vision of the Absolute will be dealt with elsewhere.[10] It is sufficient here to point out that the vision of true being is, for Plato,

[1] See Zeller, *Stoics, Epicureans, and Skeptics*, pp. 148 f., with notes.

[2] See *Timaeus* 36 D E.

[3] Bréhier, *Id. phil. et relig.*, pp. 71 f. Cf. pp. 200, 275, 296.

[4] Shorey, *The Idea of Good in Plato's Republic*, p. 188, n. 2.

[5] τὸ δὲ γενικώτατόν ἐστιν ὁ θεός, *Leg. all.* 2:86.

[6] Cf. Shorey, *Unity of Plato's Thought*, p. 16; *Idea of Good in Plato's Republic*, p. 232; *Timaeus* 44 C, 48 D.

[7] *Sophist* 248 D E; *Parm.* 141 E; contrast *Timaeus* 38 A B. See Shorey, *Unity*, p. 39.

[8] *Unity*, p. 39.

[9] Bréhier, *Id. phil. et relig.*, p. 200 and especially p. 275, n. 3. "La contemplation d'Aristote et l'extase de Platon .... sont le résultat de l'activité du sujet."

[10] See chap. v of this essay.

attained, not through intellectual activity, but in moments of divine madness, and under the influence of Eros.[1] The vision of the divine is for Plato as for Philo the vague consciousness of something infinite. We must emphasize the fact, however, that the notion of the contemplation of the divine is for both thinkers a religious concept. This does not deny that there is another aspect to the thought of both in which all the principles are exact and logical.[2]

Philo is, then, giving what is at least a plausible interpretation of Plato when he identifies God with pure being.[3] Now of pure being we can say nothing at all except that it exists.[4] We find that Philo's language in this connection reproduces the negations that characterize that of Plato. To both thinkers, God's name is unknown.[5] He is beyond perception,[6] beyond speech,[7] beyond knowledge,[8]

[1] *Phaedrus* 249 C-E; *Symp.* 211 E ff.

[2] See Shorey, *Unity*, pp. 5.f. The logical basis of Philo's thought is exhibited in the remaining parts of this essay.

[3] τὸ ὄν. See *De cherub.* 108; *Quod det. pot.* 153, 160, 161; *De post. C.* 1-4, 9, 14, 16; *Quis rer. div.* 229; *De cong.* 159; *De sac. A. et C.* 10; and many other passages. τὸ ὄν means God in Plato *Timaeus* 38 A B. See Shorey, *Unity*, p. 39. For an account of Plato's theology, see article on "Greek Philosophy" by Shorey in Hastings' *Encyc. of Religion and Ethics*, IX, 861-62.

[4] *Leg. all.* 3:206. τίς ἂν ἰσχύσαι ἢ ὅτι ἀσώματον ἢ ὅτι σῶμα ἢ ὅτι ποιὸν ἢ ὅτι ἄποιον τὸ αἴτιον εἰπεῖν ἢ συνόλως περὶ οὐσίας ἢ ποιότητος ἢ σχέσεως ἢ κινήσεως αὐτοῦ βεβαίως ἀποφήνασθαι; ἀλλὰ περὶ γε ἑαυτοῦ μόνος ἰσχυριεῖται, ἐπεὶ καὶ μόνος ἀψευδῶς τὴν ἑαυτοῦ φύσιν ἠκρίβωσε. Cf. *De post. C.* 13, 18-20; *Leg. all.* 1:91; *Quis rer. div.* 170; *Mig. Ab.* 195.

[5] *Quis rer. div.* 170; *Leg. all.* 1:91; *Somn.* 1:230. Cf. *Crat.* 400 D, περὶ θεῶν οὐδὲν ἴσμεν οὔτε περὶ αὐτῶν οὔτε περὶ ὀνομάτων, and the statement regarding the logical concept of pure being in *Parm.* 142 A, οὐδ᾽ ἄρα ὄνομα ἔστιν αὐτῷ. Philo probably regarded τὸ ὄν of the *Parmenides* as a philosophical term for God.

[6] ἀόρατον, in *Conf. ling.* 138. Cf. περὶ τὸ ὄν τε ᾖ καὶ τὸ ἀόρατον in *Rep.* 529 B and further *Tim.* 46 D; 52 A; *Soph.* 246 A B. See also *Quod Deus sit* 62, οὐδ᾽ ὡς οὐρανὸς οὐδ᾽ ὡς κόσμος· ποιὰ γὰρ εἴδη ταῦτά γε καὶ εἰς αἴσθησιν ἐρχόμενα, *Mut. nom.* 7-10; and *Fug. et Inv.* 92. With these compare *Parm.* 142 A, οὐδ᾽ ἄρα ὄνομα ἔστιν αὐτῷ . . . . οὐδὲ αἴσθησις.

[7] See ἄρρητον γὰρ τὸ ὄν in *Quis rer. div.* 170 and cf. *Mut. nom.* 15; *Leg. all.* 3:206. See *Parm.* 142 A οὐδὲ λόγος and cf. note 5 above on Philo's interpretation of the *Parmenides*.

[8] Cf. Philo, *De op. mund.* 8; *Leg. all.* 3:206; *Quod Deus sit* 109; *De post. C.* 13, 18, 168, 169; and cf. οὐδὲ τῷ νῷ καταληπτός in *Quod Deus sit* 62. In Plato, see *Parm.* 142 A, οὐδέ τις ἐπιστήμη οὐδὲ δόξα, and *Tim.* 29 C D, especially φύσιν ἀνθρωπίνην ἔχομεν, ὥστε περὶ τούτων τὸν εἰκότα μῦθον ἀποδεχομένους πρέπει τούτου μηδὲν ἔτι πέρα ζητεῖν. Also *Crat.* 400 D, *Tim.* 28 C, *Critias* 107 D and compare on the transcendence of the ideas in *Parm.* 133, *Phaedr.* 246 C D.

the unmoved[1] and unchangeable,[2] beyond time,[3] without parts[4] or form.[5]

It is by a logical contradiction that Philo attaches positive predicates to this Being of whom he has said we can know nothing. The contradiction cannot be explained away. Drummond, in his *Philo Judaeus or the Jewish Alexandrian Philosophy* (London, 1888), Vol. II, pp. 23-34, softens the meaning of ἄποιος by the logical distinction between ποιόν and ἴδιον. The word ἄποιος, he thinks, means that God is not a member of a class. It emphasizes His uniqueness but is not meant to exclude ἰδιότητας. Hence Philo can use positive language of God but this positive language is descriptive not of ποιότητας but only of ἰδιότητας. This explanation is accepted by Bréhier (*Idées phil. et relig.*, p. 72). The explanation can hardly hold in view of *Quod Deus sit* 55, where ἄποιος is explained by ψιλὴν ἄνευ χαρακτῆρος τὴν ὕπαρξιν. This latter phrase could not mean anything but the denial of the possibility of conceiving of any quality or any form in God.

We must remember, however, that the very denial of qualities to God is due to the effort to describe perfection.[6] Absolute perfection can be described only negatively. The absolute simplicity of the divine is the simplicity of a unity in which differences are transcended and united. God is, then, perfect, and in our effort to get an approximate conception of Him we have a right to attribute to Him the qualities of our ideal of perfection. Strictly speaking, such statements about God are untrue, but they are partly true. God is at least as good as the content of our human word. We get our notions of the Unbegotten, Philo tells

---

[1] See Philo *De post. C.* 19, 23, 27, 28; *Conf. ling.* 134, 139; *De gig.* 49; *Quis rer. div.* 23; for Plato see *Parm.* 139 A; *Soph.* 249 A; *Tim.* 38 A.

[2] Cf. *De plant.* 91, μένων δὲ ἐν ὁμοίῳ with *Rep.* 381 C, μένει ἀεὶ ἁπλῶς ἐν τῇ αὑτοῦ μορφῇ. For further expressions for the unchangeability of true being see Plato *Parm.* 138 C; *Rep.* 381 B C; *Parm.* 152 E; Philo *Quod Deus sit* 22; *Leg. all.* 1:51; *De plant.* 91; *Conf. ling.* 96; *De cherub.* 19, 90.

[3] *Quod Deus sit* 32, οὐ χρόνος ἀλλὰ τὸ ἀρχέτυπον τοῦ χρόνου καὶ παράδειγμα αἰὼν ὁ βίος ἐστὶν αὐτοῦ, with *Tim.* 38 B, χρόνος .... γέγονεν .... κατὰ τὸ παράδειγμα τῆς διαιωνίας φύσεως. See further in Philo, *De plant.* 51; *De post. C.* 14; *Leg. all.* 1:20; and in Plato *Parm.* 141 D E; *Tim.* 37 D ff.

[4] Philo *De gig.* 27, 52; *Leg. all.* 2:3; Plato *Soph.* 245 A; *Parm.* 137 C D.

[5] Philo *Leg. all.* 1:51; 3:36; *Quod Deus sit* 55; Plato *Parm.* 137 D; *Phaedr.* 247 C.

[6] God is not below qualities; he transcends them. See *De op. mund.* 8; *De sac. A. et C.* 10, 92, 101; *Quod Deus sit* 7; *De plant.* 51; *De cherub.* 86; *Quis rer. div.* 187; *Leg. all.* 3:10; *V.M.* 2:239. The doctrine of the perfection of God is at the basis of the theology of *Rep.* ii. See especially 379 B, 381 B. Cf. *Tim.* 29 A; *Theaet.* 176 BC.

us, from the things that happen to ourselves.[1] Although He is beyond the reach of language, we must speak of Him in words we know if we are to have any comprehension of Him at all.[2] So Plato finds it necessary to give positive determinations of God if He is to be the object of aspiration and devotion. The account we give of Him is only a probable account, an approximation to the truth.[3] Plato thinks that this must be so when we attempt to speak of any Absolute, even absolute ideas. Any terms we use are used by analogy.[4] But such language as we can use we have a right to use, even while we remember that the perfection we attempt to represent escapes and transcends all determinations.

We must remember too that this transcendent Being is the only cause,[5] the father and creator of the universe;[6] that He fills all things, not with His thought only, but with His essence.[7] True, His essence is not exhausted in the universe; He is above it and beyond.[8] Indeed we may say that only His powers are in the universe.[9] But, while He is above His powers, He includes them.[10] What they do, He does through them. Now they are visible, working in the world. From their activity we get a clue to the nature of God.[11]

[1] *Conf. ling.* 98; *De sac. A. et C.* 95 f.; and in Plato, *Phaedr.* 246 C.

[2] *Leg. ad Gai.* 6; *Mut. nom.* 13; *De Ab.* 51; *Sp. leg.* 1:209; *Somn.* 1:231 f.

[3] τὸν εἰκότα μῦθον, *Tim.* 29 D.

[4] *Parm.* 133 D. Cf. *Tim.* 29 C, μὴ δυνατοὶ γιγνώμεθα πάντῃ πάντως αὐτοὺς ἑαυτοῖς ὁμολογουμένους λόγους καὶ ἀπηκριβωμένους ἀποδοῦναι. Also *Phaedr.* 246 C.

[5] *Leg. all.* 1:20; *De cherub.* 28; *De eb.* 73, 107; *Mig. Ab.* 131; *Fug. et Inv.* 137, 141; *De post. C.* 14, 19, 168; *Quis rer. div.* 22, 114 f., 171; *Conf. ling.* 124–27. Cf. *Tim.* 29 A, *Rep.* 597 C.

[6] πατὴρ καὶ ποιητής, a phrase taken over from *Tim.* 28 C. The phrase occurs a countless number of times in Philo. The following is a partial list of the passages. *Decal.* 32, 51, 64, 90, 105, 134; *Leg. all.* 1:18, 2:49; *Mut. nom.* 45, 127; *Sp. leg.* 1:35, 96; *De op. mund.* 7; *Quis rer. div.* 62, 98, 110, 236; *Conf. ling.* 144, 170; *Mig. Ab.* 135; *Fug. et Inv.* 177, 197; *Quod Deus sit* 19, 30; *Somn.* 1:73; *V.M.* 2:48, 192, 256, 262, 288; *De Ab.* 9, 58; *Praem.* 24, 32; *Quaes. in Gen.* 1:6; *Sp. leg.* 2:6, 256; 3:127, 178, 189, 199; 4:180; *De virt.* 34, 64, 77.

[7] Cf. *supra*, p. 15, n. 3.

[8] περιέχων μὴ περιεχόμενος, *Mig. Ab.* 182–83, 192; *De post. C.* 14, 20; *De sob.* 63; *Leg. all.* 1:44, 3:51; *Conf. ling.* 136. Cf. Plato *Parm.* 138 AB, περιέχοιτο ὑπ' ἐκείνου . . . . ἕτερον . . . . τὸ περιέχον, ἕτερον δὲ τὸ περιεχόμενον.

[9] *De sac. A. et C.* 59 f.; *Mig. Ab.* 182 f.; *Mut. nom.* 15.

[10] *De op. mund.* 8; *De sac. A. et C.* 59–60.

[11] *De post. C.* 167–69; *Fug. et Inv.* 165; *Leg. all.* 1:38, 3:98 f. Cf. in Plato *Cratylus*, the naming of the gods from their powers, especially the phraseology in *Crat.* 405 A and 405 E.

The ideal of perfection set forth by Philo is in striking accord with that of Plato. The chief points emphasized are the unchangeability of God in contrast to the changing things of sense;[1] the perfect goodness of God,[2] a goodness which means a fatherly care for men and for all creation; His perfect knowledge and power. In repeating these ideas, Philo makes constant use of Platonic phraseology. The following list of parallels reveals his close relationship to Plato.

δεσπότης: used of God in Plato *Phaedo*, 62 D. Cf. θεοὺς ὄντας δεσπότας in *Laws* 726.

See in Philo *De cherub.* 83, 107; *Quis rer. div.* 23; *De plant.* 53.

ἡγεμών: used of Love in Plato *Symp.* 197 E. Cf. τὸν τῶν πάντων θεὸν ἡγεμόνα τῶν τε ὄντων καὶ τῶν μελλόντων in the pseudo-Platonic Epistle VI, 323 C, with Shorey's note, *Class. Phil.*, X, 87 f.

Philo *De sac. A. et C.* 129; *De plant.* 2; *Quis rer. div.* 7; *De cherub.* 99, 107, 108; *Quod det. pot.* 29, 155; *De post. C.* 5, 9; *Quod Deus sit* 19; *Sp. leg.* 1:32.

βασιλεύς: Plato *Crat.* 396 A, ἄρχων τε καὶ βασιλεὺς τῶν πάντων; *Laws* 904 A; 905 E.

Philo *De post C.* 101; *De gig.* 46; *De ag.* 51, 78; *De plant.* 33, 92; *Cong.* 116; *De op. mund.* 88; *Mig. Ab.* 146; *Fug. et Inv.* 66, 95, 98; *Conf. ling.* 170; *De cherub.* 99.

κυβερνήτης: Plato *Laws* 905 E–906 E; *Pol.* 272 E; *Symp.* 197 E.

Philo *Conf. ling.* 98; *De op. mund.* 46.

νομοθέτης: Plato *Laws* 662 C, τοὺς νομοθετήσαντες .... θεούς.

Philo *Fug. et Inv.* 66, 95, 99.

φιλόδωρος: Plato, used of Love in *Symp.* 197 D.

Philo *De post. C.* 26; *Fug. et Inv.* 62, 66.

φιλάνθρωπος: Plato *Laws* 713 D, ὁ θεός ἄρα καὶ φιλάνθρωπος ὤν. Cf. on Love in *Symp.* 189 D.

Philo *De plant.* 92; *De cherub.* 99; *De post. C.* 147.

διδάσκαλος: Plato on Love in *Symp.* 197 A, οὐ μὲν ἂν ὁ θεὸς οὗτος διδάσκαλος γένηται.

Philo *De op. mund.* 149; *Cong.* 114; *Leg. all.* 3:162, 163; *Quis rer. div.* 19, 25, 67, 102; *Mig. Ab.* 15.

σωτήρ: Plato *Tim.* 48 D, σωτῆρα ἐξ ἀτόπου καὶ ἀήθους διηγήσεως. Cf. σωτὴρ ἄριστος of Love in *Symp.* 197 D E.

Philo *De sac. A. et C.* 70; *Quod Deus sit* 156; *Quis rer. div.* 60; *Fug. et Inv.* 162; *Mig. Ab.* 25; *De sob.* 55; *Cong.* 171; *De op. mund.* 169; *De post. C.* 156; *Conf. ling.* 93; *Sp. leg.* 2:198.

[1] See above, p. 18, n. 2.   [2] See p. 18, n. 6.

PHILO'S CONCEPTION OF THE ULTIMATE REALITY 21

ἐπιστάτης: Plato *Phaedo* 62 D, οἵπερ ἄριστοί εἰσιν τῶν ὄντων ἐπιστάται, θεοί; *Pol.* 271 E; *Symp.* 197 D.
    Philo *Quod. det. pot.* 142. Cf. ἐπίτροπος, *Cong.* 118; *Quod Deus sit.* 30; κηδεμών, *Cong.* 118.

εὐμενής: Plato *Laws* 712 B.
    Philo *Quod det. pot.* 95.

Cause of good only: Plato *Tim.* 29 E–30 A, 42 D E, *Rep.* 379 B C, 380 C, 617 E.
    Philo *De plant.* 53; *Conf. ling.* 179; *De ag.* 129 f.; *Fug. et Inv.* 79, 80. Cf. εὐεργέτης in *De sob.* 55; *De plant.* 86–89; *De op. mund.* 169; *Cong.* 171; *De post. C.* 154.

ἵλεως: Plato *Laws* 792 D, 712 B. Cf. praise of Love in *Symp.* 197 D.
    Philo *Mig. Ab.* 15, 124; *Fug. et Inv.* 141; *De plant.* 90.

ἀγένητος: Plato *Phaedr.* 245 D, *Rep.* 527 B.
    Philo *Conf. ling.* 98; *De virt.* 65, 213; *De decal.* 41, 64; *De cherub.* 44; *De gig.* 42; *Quod Deus sit* 56; *Leg. all.* 1:51.

ἀΐδιος: Plato *Tim.* 37 E.
    Philo *De decal.* 41, 64; *De op. mund.* 12; *De virt.* 65. Cf. ἄφθαρτος, *Leg. all.* 1:51; 2:3.

Perfectly just: Philo *Fug. et Inv.* 82, quoting Plato *Theaet.* 176 C.

The beginning and the ending: Plato *Laws* 715 E. ὁ . . . . θεὸς . . . . ἀρχήν τε καὶ τελευτὴν καὶ μέσα τῶν ὄντων ἁπάντων ἔχων.
    Philo *Quis rer. div.* 120, καὶ μὴν ὥσπερ αἱ ἀρχαὶ θεοῦ, οὕτως καὶ τὰ τέλη θεοῦ.

Wise: Plato *Laws* 902 E; *Tim.* 51 E; *Phaedr.* 278 D.
    Philo *Mig. Ab.* 134; *Cong.* 114; *Fug. et Inv.* 47; *De sac. A. et C.* 120.

Physician: Plato *Pol.* 273 E; *Laws* 903 BC, 905 E; *Symp.* 189 D.
    Philo *De sac. A. et C.* 70; *Mig. Ab.* 124.

The figure of the sun in Plato, *Rep.* 508, there applied to the Idea of Good, is a frequent figure in Philo to represent God. He is the sun of the intelligible world (*De Ab.* 119). Philo carries the analogy farther than Plato does. For example, he says that just as the physical sun dazzles by its brightness, so the glory of God dazzles our minds (*Sp. leg.* 1:37–40).[1]

But Philo by no means confines himself to the vocabulary of Plato. The philosophical and religious sects had developed a considerable range

---

[1] For further illustrations of the use of the figure, see *Somn.* 1:72–76, 90 f., 112; *De praem.* 37–39, 45 f.; *Sp. leg.* 1:279; *De virt.* 164, 179; Frg. from J. of D. 748 B (M. 654); *De cherub.* 97; *Fug. et Inv.* 136.

of expression since Plato's day and Philo seems to use the language of many schools of set purpose in order to commend to those who had been influenced by those schools the opinions he upholds. Stoic vocabulary is freely drawn upon. God is, for example, called the active cause, τὸ δραστήριον αἴτιον.[1] The expression δραστήριον does not occur in Plato, though κινοῦν, which Philo uses in *Fug. et Inv.* 8, is a Platonic equivalent (*Phaedrus* 245 D E). But even while using the Stoic word, Philo does not depart from his essential Platonism. In attributing all perfection to God, Philo uses at times expressions which describe the perfect man. In several passages, God is called blessed and happy, a phrase used in Plato to describe the ideal life.[2] Expressions that describe the Stoic wise man are freely applied to God.[3] Aristotle is drawn upon for the idea that God is beyond the reach of praise.[4] The language of unrestrained adulation found in the addresses to the Hellenistic kings and emperors shows many parallels to Philo's characterization of God.[5] The term τριπόθητος which is twice used[6] is a hint of Philo's adoption of the vocabulary of the cults of his native Alexandria. But through all this variety of expression, the one thought of God's perfection and beneficence is repeated and emphasized.

The word πατήρ is used of God, not only in the physical sense in which the word is used in Plato, but with the moral implications of the word developed. In the *De Jos.* 265, God is contrasted with our earthly father and is said to be "the unbegotten, incorruptible, everlasting Father, who sees all things and hears all things, even the things that are

[1] *De op. mund.* 8; *De cherub.* 87; *Quod det. pot.* 162; *Fug. et Inv.* 11.

[2] Plato *Rep.* 354 A, *Laws* 660 E, 730 C, *Gorg.* 507 C. Expression applied to God in Philo *De plant.* 35; *Quod Deus sit* 108; *De Ab.* 87; *Sp. leg.* 1:209, 329; 2:53.

[3] ὁ μόνος σοφός, *Mig. Ab.* 134; *Cong.* 114; *Fug. et Inv.* 47; *De sac. A. et C.* 120. ὁ μόνος ἐλεύθερος, *Quis rer. div.* 186; *Somn.* 2:243. ὁ μόνος πολίτης, *De cherub.* 121. ὁ μόνος βασιλεύς, *De post. C.* 101; *Cong.* 116; *Mig. Ab.* 146; *Conf. ling.* 170. For similar expressions applied to the Stoic wise man see Zeller, *Stoics, Epicureans, and Skeptics*, p. 270 with notes.

[4] *Leg. all.* 3:10. Cf. *V.M.* 2(3):239; *Mig. Ab.* 40. In Aristotle *Eth. Nic.* 1101 b 22, virtue is declared to be beyond praise, since praise implies the existence of a standard beyond the object praised. In *De sac. A. et C.* 34 Philo declares that virtue needs no praise. Like the sun and the moon, it is its own best evidence.

[5] See Wendland, *Die Hell. Röm. Kultur*, pp. 76 f.; pp. 100–103. Note the phrases μέγας βασιλεύς αἰωνόβιος, the names Σωτήρ, Εὐεργέτης in the Rosetta inscription (p. 77); σωτῆρα καὶ εὐεργέτην (p. 100–101); κοινὸν τοῦ ἀνθρωπίνου βίου σωτῆρα used of Augustus. See Dittenberger, *Sylloge Inscript. Graec.* (Leipzig, 1898), Vol. I, No. 347.

[6] *De post. C.* 12; *Mut. nom.* 7. Cf. τριπόθητος Ἄδωνις, quotation from a hymn in Hippolytus, *Refut. omn. Haen.* 5:9.

PHILO'S CONCEPTION OF THE ULTIMATE REALITY 23

quiet, the one who always sees even the things that are in the inmost recesses of the soul." The ideas here attached to the word come from Aristotle, *Eth. Nic.* 1160 b, 24 f.: ἡ μὲν γὰρ πατρὸς πρὸς υἱεῖς κοινωνία βασιλείας ἔχει σχῆμα· τῶν τέκνων γὰρ τῷ πατρὶ μέλει. ἐντεῦθεν δὲ καὶ Ὅμηρος τὸν Δία πατέρα προσαγορεύει· πατρικὴ γὰρ ἀρχὴ βούλεται ἡ βασιλεία εἶναι. The Homeric passage referred to is *Il.* 15.47, πατὴρ ἀνδρῶν τε θεῶν τε. The same phrase is used in Hesiod, *Shield of Heracles* 27, with a notion of fatherly care.

πατὴρ δ' ἀνδρῶν τε θεῶν τε
ἄλλην μῆτιν ὕφαινε μετὰ φρεσίν, ὄφρα θεοῖσιν
ἀνδράσι τ' ἀλφηστῆσιν ἀρῆς ἀλκτῆρα φυτεύσαι.

The notion of God's providential care is emphasized in Plato, though it does not occur in connection with the word πατήρ. See especially *Laws* 899 D ff., and Professor Shorey's article on "Greek Philosophy" in Hastings' *Encyclopedia of Religion and Ethics*, IX, 861–62.

While this use of πατήρ implies that all men are God's children, there are certain passages in which Philo speaks as if only the wise man were the son of God.[1] So in *Conf. ling.* 145, he interprets the expression υἱοὶ θεοῦ in Deut. 14:1 as equivalent to οἱ δὲ ἐπιστήμῃ κεχρημένοι τοῦ ἑνός. In *De sob.* 56 the wise man is described as μόνος εὐγενής since he has God as his Father. Sonship to God is here equivalent to the mystic ὁμοίωσις, a familiar idea in the Greek mystery religions.[2]

Over against the perfect, unchangeable Being, Plato had set in his thought the world of change and decay in which we live. This world is in constant flux.[3] Evil is due to the fact that the world of matter by its very nature does not receive the motions of order but moves in confusion.[4] This teaching is also that of Philo. This world is to him, too, a world of constant flux, where things are wavering and uncertain,[5] where evil clings to us by the very fact that we are on the earth and bound to becoming.[6]

[1] See Bréhier, *Id. phil. et relig.*, p. 234.

[2] For ὁμοίωσις, see Plato *Theaet.* 176 B–C; *Rep.* 500 C; *Phaedr.* 613 A–252 E, and compare Vergil *Ecl.* iv, "ille deum vitam accipiet," with Conington's note in Vol. III, p. 518 of his edition of Vergil; Rohde, *Psyche*, II, 14 ff.

[3] *Phaedo* 78 D E; *Symp.* 207 E, 208 A; *Crat.* 439 D.

[4] *Tim.* 46 E; 47 E–48 A.

[5] *Sp. leg.* 1:27; 3:178; *Quod det. pot.* 148; *De post. C.* 23, 29; *Quod Deus sit* 4; 119 f.; *Fug. et Inv.* 160; *Frg.* M. 674; *Mut. nom.* 156; *De cherub.* 19; *Cong.* 107; *De Ab.* 84; *Somn.* 2:253, 258.

[6] *Quod det. pot.* 146; *Quaes. in Gen.* 4:157, 365; *De plant.* 53; *Conf. ling.* 106, 177; *Quis rer. div.* 240; *De eb.* 208.

Philo's Platonism has been generally recognized in connection with his doctrine of matter,[1] and the subject need not detain us here. Matter in his system is completely passive, without quality or motion, capable under the influence of divine power of becoming anything and everything in sensible existence, but of itself dead and formless.[2] The language used is borrowed from Plato's description of primary matter.[3] Primary matter is, for Philo and for Plato alike, uncreated, a kind of eternal being.[4] Both authors in describing primal matter so emphasize its nothingness in comparison with God that all notions are abstracted from it except that of extension,[5] though Philo does not identify primal matter with space so explicitly as Plato does. Both authors, again, while they think of primal matter as qualified only by extension, are unable, in picturing creation, to escape the notion of a pre-cosmic chaos.[6] Here too the difference is that Plato is more explicit than Philo. He definitely posits a secondary matter. He does not tell us how the change from primary to secondary matter takes place but only that "the nurse of becoming, made moist and fiery, and receiving the shapes of earth and air and undergoing all the other changes that accompany these becomes manifold in appearance." It becomes filled with powers that are unequal and unbalanced, and by reason of this unequal distribution of weight it is shaken in every part. By this motion, the various

---

[1] For a discussion of Philo's views see Bréhier, *Id. phil.*, p. 81; Drummond, *Philo Jud.*, I, 299–306; Baümker, *Problem der Materie*, p. 384; Robins, *Hexaemeral Lit.*, Chicago Diss. (1912), p. 30, n. 4; Zeller, *Phil. der Griech.*, Vol. III, Part II, p. 387.

[2] *De op. mund.* 9, 22; *Quis rer. div.* 140, 160; called "mother and nurse of created things," *De eb.* 61.

[3] *Tim.* 30 A, 50 CD, 51 A. Cf. for "mother" *Tim.* 50 D, 51 A; for "nurse" *Tim.* 49 A; 52 D.

[4] Cf. Shorey, *AJP*, X, 48, note to *Tim.* 30 A. Philo nowhere speaks of matter as created. Passages which seem to imply that it is created are pointed out by Keferstein (*Philos Lehre v. d. göttl. Mittel*, Leipzig, 1846, p. 6), Grossmann (*Quaes. Phil.*, I, 19, n. 70), and Siegfried (*Philo v. Alex.*, pp. 232 f.). Heinze follows Siegfried. See his *Lehre von Logos*, p. 210, note. These passages have been correctly interpreted by Drummond, *loc. cit.* They are *Somn.* 1:76 (οὐ μόνον δημιουργὸς ἀλλὰ καὶ κτιστής). Frg. from Eusebius (M ii. 325 f.); *De Deo* (M. 616). Other passages clearly imply the independent existence of matter. See *De op. mund.* 9; *Quaes. in Gen.* 1:55; *Somn.* 2:45; *Sp. leg.* 1:329. So Baümker, Bréhier, Robins.

[5] For Philo see *De op. mund.* 9, ἄψυχον, ἀκίνητον; *Fug. et Inv.* 8 f., ἄποιον καὶ ἀνείδεον καὶ ἀσχημάτιστον οὐσίαν. Cf. *Fug. et Inv.* 198; *Mut. nom.* 135; *Somn.* 2:45; *Sp. leg.* 1:328; 4:187; *Quaes. in Gen.* 1:55. For Plato see Shorey in *AJP*, IX, 298.

[6] Cf. *De plant.* 3; *Somn.* 2:45; *Sp. leg.* 1:328; 2:151; and in Plato *Tim.* 30 A and 50 C.

elements are separated "even before the universe was formed out of them." But they all existed without reason or order, disposed just as one would expect when God was not there.[1] The universe was not quiet, but moving without harmony or order.[2]

Zeller thinks that Philo's use of the word οὐσία for matter means that he here adopts a Stoic point of view opposed to that of Plato. The expression, he says, is identical with "body" in the Stoic teaching and by using it Philo seems to imply "against Plato and with the Stoics" a material substratum.[3] But Plato did believe in a material substratum. Zeller identifies space in Plato with the μὴ ὄν and does not recognize that this "primary matter" is, in the *Timaeus*, a kind of eternal being.[4] In *Timaeus* 52 C, Plato actually says that phenomena cling to οὐσία through their existence in space. The use of the word οὐσία to designate this material substratum is, however, not Platonic. The Stoics used the word for matter, defining this as Plato defined ὄν in *Sophist* 247 DE. For them, οὐσία was that which could act and be acted upon.[5] It is an interesting case of the way in which the vocabulary of Stoicism influences Philo, even when he does not accept their thought, that he adopts their term for real existence and transfers it to his notion of matter, the completely passive substratum. He is as far as possible from accepting the Stoic idea that matter could ever be the active cause.

[1] *Tim.* 52 D–53 B.

[2] *Tim.* 30 A. Philo does not admit movement without νοῦς. Cf. *De op. mund.* 9, κινηθὲν δὲ καὶ σχηματισθὲν καὶ ψυχωθὲν ὑπὸ τοῦ νοῦ, with *Tim.* 50 C, κινούμενον καὶ διασχηματιζόμενον ὑπὸ τῶν εἰσιόντων. Bréhier, *Id. phil.*, p. 79, regards *De op. mund.* 9, ἄψυχον καὶ ἀκίνητον ἐξ ἑαυτοῦ, as an explicit contradiction of *Tim.* 30 A. But for Plato too the *primary* matter is moved ὑπὸ τῶν εἰσιόντων and is perfectly without qualities. See *Tim.* 50 D E; 51 A B.

[3] *Phil. der Griech.*, Vol. III, Part II, p. 387.

[4] See Shorey, *Unity*, pp. 38, 39.

[5] Passages quoted in Zeller, *Stoics, Epicureans, and Skeptics*, p. 126, n. 2.

CHAPTER III

THE INTERMEDIARY POWERS

Between God and creation, mediating God's activity in the world, Philo has described a series of beings arranged in varying hierarchies. Here, as elsewhere, one school of interpretation has found bits of Stoic, Heraclitean, neo-Pythagorean, Platonic, and Oriental mystic teaching mingled together without any effort to discover and state the principle which gives to all of these their unity of content.[1] And here, as elsewhere, it is the breadth of Philo's learning, the eclecticism of his style, which has misled scholars. He permits himself to use the expressions of many schools without departing at all from the unity and consistency of his own thought. The clue to his thought here too is Platonism, the mingling in Plato of sound, consistent, logical thought with the fervor and imagination of the religious teacher and maker of myths. These two elements are present in Philo's teaching. They are not so clearly and explicitly distinguished as they are in Plato, but we are by no means left without a clue to Philo's consciousness of the two sides of his teaching.

A great source of difficulty to the student of Philo's thought in this connection is the ambiguity of the word λόγος.[2] It may mean "the mind," or "faculty of thought," and so be equivalent to νοῦς or διάνοια.[3] Again, it may mean "an idea in the mind."[4] Still another meaning is that of "right reason" or "reasonableness."[5] In countless passages it means simply "speech."[6] Other non-technical meanings that occur in Philo are "account," "definition," "essay," "principle."[7]

This brief summary is sufficient to indicate that the expression λόγος θεοῦ has to be examined carefully in relation to its context before we

---

[1] So especially Bréhier, *Id. phil. et relig.*, pp. 83-111.

[2] Grossmann, *Quaes. Philon.*, II, 3 ff. has classified the meanings. There is a brief discussion in Drummond, *Phil. Jud.*, II, 156 ff. Only typical passages are given in the present essay.

[3] *De op. mund.* 24. In this sense the Logos might be called a δύναμις of God. Cf. *Mut. nom.* 14 f. where it seems to be so identified. Cf. Bréhier, *op. cit.*, p. 113.

[4] *Mig. Ab.* 71.

[5] *Fug. et Inv.* 137; *V.M.* 2:52; *Jos.* 174; *Somn.* 2:223 (where λόγος is identified with the νόμος of God).

[6] *Mig. Ab.* 71. Cf. the common reference to scripture passages as λόγοι θεοῦ.

[7] "Account," cf. λόγον ἀποδοῦναι, *Quod det. pot.* 43; "definition," *Quod Deus sit* 167; "essay," *De op. mund.* 52; "principle," *De op. mund.* 43, 48.

THE INTERMEDIARY POWERS

assign to it a specific meaning. The expression is sometimes used in a non-technical sense as "God's faculty of thought." So in *De op. mund.* 20 the ideal universe is said to exist only in the λόγος of God.[1] Closely akin to this is its use as equivalent to the product of God's thought, an idea in the mind of God. In *De op. mund.* 24, Philo says "if we abandon all metaphor (εἰ δέ τις ἐθελήσειε γυμνοτέροις χρήσασθαι τοῖς ὀνόμασιν) the ideal world is just the λόγος of God when He is in the act of fashioning the universe. The ideal universe is nothing else than the thought (λογισμός) of the architect just when he is deciding to found the city."[2]

Horowitz[3] has failed to notice that λόγος here is used, not in its technical, metaphorical sense, but is parallel with λογισμός, and means not "the Logos," but "the thought." All the passage can suggest is that God's thought, His λογισμός, is not completely expressed in creation. It does not mean that the κόσμος νοητός is to be regarded as a limited aspect of the Logos, but that the Logos is a limited aspect of God—God, that is to say, in His creative aspect. Philo is convinced that even in the ideal cosmos we see only such an aspect of God's thought as is capable of being expressed in material form. This is, as Horowitz points out, the meaning of the passage in *De op. mund.* 21–25 on the transcendent goodness of God, of which the passage just quoted forms the conclusion. Drummond[4] is wrong when he says "there is only one cosmos and its ideal is exhaustive of the divine thought."

The particular λόγος, or thought, which is in the mind of God when He is in the act of fashioning the universe, is the idea of the universe in the Platonic sense of the term. "The archetypal seal," Philo tells us, "would itself be the λόγος of God."[5] In the metaphorical language of feeling and under the influence of the religious imagination, this idea is endowed with personality.[6] It becomes a god; not a cold,

[1] Cf. *De op. mund.* 36.
[2] Cf. *Tim.* 34 A, οὗτος δὴ πᾶς ὄντος ἀεὶ λογισμὸς θεοῦ περὶ τὸν ποτὲ ἐσόμενον θεὸν λογισθεὶς λεῖον καὶ ὁμαλὸν πανταχῇ τε ἐκ μέσου ἴσον καὶ ὅλον καὶ τέλεον ἐκ τελέων σωμάτων σῶμα ἐποίησεν.
[3] *Das platonische Νοητὸν Ζῷον und der philonische Κόσμος Νοητός* (Marburg, 1900), pp. 83 ff.
[4] Drummond, *Phil. Jud.*, II, 177.
[5] *De op. mund.* 25. Cf. *Fug. et Inv.* 12; *Leg. all.* 1:19–21, 3:96; *Conf. ling.* 97; *Somn.* 2:45; *Mig. Ab.* 103.
[6] For a discussion of the personality of the Logos see Drummond, *Phil. Jud.*, II, 222–73; Heinze, *Lehre v. Logos*, pp. 291–94. As Heinze points out, *Somn.* 1:127 f. is decisive for the personality of the Logos. Other significant passages are *Somn.* 1:230; *Leg. all.* 3:207; Frg. from Eusebius (M., p. 625).

abstract principle, but a living being and the object of aspiration and desire.[1]

The word λόγοι covers just the same varied conceptions as we have found in λόγος. The λόγοι are primarily thoughts in the mind of God,[2] or phases of the divine activity.[3] They are Philo's equivalent for the ideas of Plato. Under the influence of the religious imagination they are hypostatized and endowed with personality.[4] But they remain thoughts of God. Thus we are told that God and the two supreme powers are a threefold appearance of one reality.[5] It is not a part of Philo's philosophical system to regard them as living beings.

The tendency to personify the ideas is to be found in Plato. In *Timaeus* 37 C the ideas seem to be called θεοί and to be personified. See Shorey's note on this passage in *AJP*, X, 56. Dr. Shorey compares σφαίρας αὐτῆς τῆς θείας in *Phileb.* 62 A and *Polit.* 309 C, where true opinion in the soul is θείαν . . . . ἐν δαιμονίῳ γένει. Compare *Epinomis* 983 E–984 A: ἢ γὰρ θεοὺς αὐτοὺς ταῦτα ὑμνητέον ὀρθότατα, ἢ θεῶν εἰκόνας ὡς ἀγάλματα ὑπολαβεῖν γεγονέναι, θεῶν αὐτῶν ἐργασαμένων.

In order to understand the thought of Philo, we must disregard the language of metaphor and think of these beings as thoughts of God or modes of His activity. We must remember, however, that for the religious imagination they are persons.[6] If any distinction is made between angels and powers in *Conf. ling.* 171 ff., it is that the powers are ideal counterparts of the angels, or higher angels belonging more to the ideal world. But this distinction is not preserved. Angels are

---

[1] *Somn.* 1:66, 68–71; *Conf. ling.* 147 f.; *Quis rer. div.* 205 f.

[2] This explains *De post. C.* 89 ff.

[3] δυνάμεις: *Somn.* 1:69 f. Identified with ideas, *Sp. leg.* 1:45–49. For the underlying meaning of δυνάμεις as "powers" note *Somn.* 1:77; *Quis rer. div.* 43, 73; *Somn.* 2:145, 151, 215; *De Ab.* 29 f., 57, 73; *De virt.* 13, 26, 33; *Conf. ling.* 111; *Mig. Ab.* 119; *De plant.* 30 f., 83 f. where the word describes functions or modes of activity of the human soul.

[4] *Conf. ling.* 171 ff.; *De post. C.* 89 ff. where angels are defined as οἱ πρὸ ἡμῶν καὶ παντὸς τοῦ γεώδους πρεσβύτεροι λόγοι καὶ θεῖοι and are said to "fix the boundaries of virtue." Cf. *De plant.* 14 where δυνάμεις and ἄγγελοι are used interchangeably. Cf. *Mig. Ab.* 173; *Conf. ling.* 28; *Somn.* 1:146–48, 190; 2:185 f. In *Somn.* 1:134–43 the beings that people the air are called λόγοι. The description tallies with that of ψυχαί or δυνάμεις in *De gig.* 6 ff., and angels in *De plant.* 14 ff.

[5] *De Ab.* 122. Cf. *De op. mund.* 23; *De plant.* 86 f. So in *Sp. leg.* 1:209, the "logos" about God admits of διαίρεσις according to His δυνάμεις and virtues.

[6] Drummond, *Phil. Jud.*, II, 222–73 goes too far in denying personality to the Logoi.

called λόγοι in *Mig. Ab.* 173, and *Conf. ling.* 28. The λόγοι have the functions of angels in *Somn.* 2:186, where they are called ἐπίσκοποι καὶ ἔφοροι τῶν τῆς φύσεως πραγμάτων, and in *Somn.* 1:146-48, where they are said to aid the soul to rise to the higher life. In *Somn.* 1:134-43, Logoi are described exactly as are angels in *De plant.* 14 ff. and powers in *De gig.* 6 ff. Powers and Logoi are identified in *Somn.* 1:69 ff.

This brief discussion makes it clear how we should interpret the inclusion of the Logos among souls in *Somn.* 1:127 f., a passage which Heinze[1] regards as furnishing decisive proof for the view that Philo seriously regarded the Logos as a person. "The divine place, the holy country, is full of incorporeal λόγοι. These λόγοι are immortal souls. Of these Logoi He takes one, choosing as the best the highest one, one which is, so to speak, the head of the united body, and gives it a firm foundation near His own thought (διάνοια)." The personification is purely mythical. The Logos is one of God's thoughts, the supreme one, it is true, but still one among others and so not to be regarded as completely exhaustive of His διάνοια. The identification of λόγοι with ψυχαί should cause no difficulty, especially as Heinze, in the context of the passage cited, points out the possibility of interpreting the words angel[2] and archangel[3] when used to describe the Logos as metaphorical or mythical expressions.

It is, then, with conscious use of metaphor and myth that Philo speaks of the Logos and Logoi as personal. It is unfair to interpret, as Zeller has done,[4] the fluctuation of Philo's expression between the notions of personality and non-personality as the violent effort of a thinker who regards God as completely transcendent to bring Him somehow into relation with the world. Zeller thinks that for Philo the transcendence is preserved by regarding the Logoi as personal, while immanence is attained by regarding them as mere phases of God's activity. This is true as far as it goes, but it should be added that it is with conscious use of myth that Philo adopts this way of speaking. Philo is here laboring under the same difficulty that all believers in an Absolute have to face. We cannot attain to God Himself. God Himself cannot come into relation with the world of change. Yet somehow, if He is to be a God at all, He must do so. How He does is an unsolved mystery. Only some such violent method as Philo has adopted, some

[1] *Lehre v. Logos*, pp. 292 f.
[2] *De cherub.* 3. 35; *Mut. nom.* 87; *Fug. et Inv.* 5; *Quod Deus sit* 182.
[3] *Conf. ling.* 146. Cf. Drummond, *Phil. Jud.*, II, 239-43.
[4] *Phil. der Griech.*, Vol. III, Part II, pp. 378 f.

mystical and metaphorical use of language, can serve to give an appearance of reconciling these two necessary aspects of an Absolute which yet enters into relations with the universe.

The personality of the Logos is not, then, the aspect which affords the clue to its meaning in Philo's system. The Logos is primarily the idea of the universe. The name which Philo adopts for this metaphysical entity was probably current in his day in many schools of speculation. It had been made popular by the Stoic thinkers who, taking it over from Heraclitus, used it as the designation of the reason or law of the universe. As such, it is in their system equivalent to God, the supreme divinity. In Stoic speculations, this reason or law is generative and is the sum of those forces which have produced the universe and the individual things in it. These forces are material.

But in spite of the materialism to which the Stoic monism led, their doctrine of the Logos has close affinities with the Platonic Idea of Good and is, in fact a development from it. Both are, in their respective systems, logical and ethical first principles, both are represented as the cause of all that exists, both are hypostatized and become the objects of aspiration and desire. These affinities will be clear if we trace the development of the notion from Plato through Aristotle to the Stoics.

In dialectics, the Idea of Good in the *Republic*[1] is the ἀρχὴν ἀνυπόθετον, the first principle, which is axiomatic, beyond which we cannot go in any discussion. No discussion is possible unless the persons who are to carry it on agree on some first principle. The dialectician, however, is always ready to reject this provisional ἀρχή or hypothesis and fall back on one that is still more fundamental. He is willing to go in this way as far as he needs (ἐπὶ τὸ ἱκανόν). Theoretically, there must be a final ἀρχή which is not a mere provisional hypothesis but is the truth beyond all question. This ἀρχὴ ἀνυπόθετος is the Good "so far as we assume that idea to be attainable in ethics or physics." Again, in studying conduct, we find that one thing is loved for the sake of another; but, if we follow back this series of ends far enough, we come to the ἀγαθόν or πρῶτον φίλον, the ultimate Good. So in the sphere of physical science Plato believes that the true explanation of each thing is its purpose, the good it is meant to accomplish. But this particular good is a means to a larger good and finally we come to the all-inclusive Good, an aim great enough to comprehend in itself all those subordinate aims which are the

---

[1] *Rep.* 504 E ff. See Shorey, *Idea of Good in Plato's Republic*, "Studies in Classical Philology" (Chicago, 1895), I, 188–259, especially 230 ff.

cause of the existence of all that is. The Good is, then, the end of controversy in physics and in ethics, the ἀρχὴ ἀνυπόθετον.

In their choice of the word Logos as the designation of this ultimate reality, the Stoics were, as has been mentioned above, primarily influenced by Heraclitus. But Aristotle's use of the phrase ὀρθὸς λόγος to designate the ethical ideal helped to determine the content they gave it. This expression is used in a non-technical sense in Plato (*Critias* 109 B), οὐ γὰρ ἂν ὀρθὸν ἔχοι λόγον θεοὺς ἀγνοεῖν τὰ πρέποντα, where ὀρθὸν ἔχοι λόγον means "it would not be a true account." Compare for the same meaning *Laws* 890 D. The expression also occurs in *Phaedo* 94 A in a sense which is slightly different. The words are κατὰ τὸν ὀρθὸν λόγον κακίας οὐδεμία ψυχὴ μεθέξει. Here, used with the article, it means "the right account." In *Phaedo* 73 A, it is already, as it is in Aristotle, moving toward its later technical meaning. The passage reads καίτοι εἰ μὴ ἐτύγχανεν αὐτοῖς ἐπιστήμη ἐνοῦσα καὶ ὀρθὸς λόγος and the expression is equivalent to "true judgment."[1] So also *Polit.* 310 C.

Aristotle[2] (*Eth. Nic.* 1103 b 32), speaks as if the phrase was used in a half-technical sense by some ethical school. "The doctrine that virtue is an activity in accordance with ὀρθὸς λόγος is one which we hold in common with other schools (κοινόν), and may be assumed as our hypothesis."[3] Here ὀρθὸς λόγος should be translated as "the right account."[4] In 1144 b 27 virtue is said to be not only κατὰ τὸν ὀρθὸν λόγον but μετὰ τοῦ ὀρθοῦ λόγου. That is, virtue is not merely subject to ὀρθὸς λόγος as an external guiding force, but it has ὀρθὸς λόγος as the inner principle of its activity. "And," Aristotle adds, "ὀρθὸς λόγος περὶ τῶν τοιούτων ἡ φρόνησίς ἐστιν." I think we should translate this "wisdom par excellence, the wisdom of the ethical philosophers, consists in right thinking on matters of this kind." Burnet, in his note on this passage (p. 286 of his edition), denies that ὀρθὸς λόγος is an ἀρετή or identical with φρόνησις. He explains the passage as meaning that the ὀρθὸς λόγος of action may be regarded as the form of goodness existing in the soul of the φρόνιμος and identical with the φρόνησις of the man who has the λόγος. But this is just what φρόνησις is, according to the definition in 1140 a 24 f. "Regarding φρόνησις, we should get a definition of it by considering whom we call the φρόνιμοι. It seems that the φρόνιμος

[1] For the passage from *Phaedo* see Burnet, *Phaedo*, pp. 73 and 94.

[2] For λόγος in Aristotle see Heinze, *op. cit.*, pp. 75–78.

[3] Burnet, *The Ethics of Aristotle*, p. 79, says that the doctrine is κοινόν since it comes from the Academy. Cf. *Eth. Nic.* 1144 b 21 and Burnet's note there (p. 286 of his edition).

[4] Cf. also 1114 b 29. Burnet says "the right rule"; so also Grant.

is one who has the ability to make proper judgments regarding what is good and advantageous for himself, not in any one part of life, as for example in the sphere of health or strength, but in the field of a good life generally." Moreover the whole context of the passage in 1144 b shows that ἡ φρόνησις is the φρόνησις of the ethical schools, not φρόνησις in any limited sense. If one makes a distinction between ὁ ὀρθὸς λόγος and φρόνησις, it would be the distinction implied in Aristotle's words in 1144 b 23, ὀρθὸς δ' ὁ κατὰ τὴν φρόνησιν. φρόνησις is, that is to say, a ἕξις, and ὀρθὸς λόγος an ἐνέργεια.[1] But this distinction is not maintained.[2]

There is another passage which is important for Aristotle's conception of ὀρθὸς λόγος. He says in *Eth. Nic.* 1138 b 21 ff.:

In all the states of the soul we have mentioned, and in all the rest as well, there is a mark to which the man who has the λόγος looks when he tightens or loosens the tension and a definition in some sort of the means which, according to our statement, are between the excess and the defect, means which, we said, are according to the ὀρθὸς λόγος. Such a statement is true enough but it is not clear. For in other pursuits which are capable of being scientifically described it is true to say that we must not toil or rest either too much or too little but between the two extremes and according to the ὀρθὸς λόγος. But a man who had merely this to guide him would be none the wiser, for example, as regards the treatment he should give his body, if one should say that he ought to treat it as the science of medicine and the one who has it bids. And so we must have, regarding the habits of the soul, not merely this statement we have made, true as it is, but a clear statement as to what ὁ ὀρθὸς λόγος is and a sort of definition of it.

ὁ ὀρθὸς λόγος is, then, as the comparison with the science of medicine shows, the scientific formulation of ethical truth in the mind of the expert. Compare, after Burnet, *Met.* 1070 a 29, ἡ γὰρ ἰατρικὴ ὁ λόγος τῆς ὑγιείας ἐστίν, and 1070 b 32, ὑγίεια γάρ πως.ἡ ἰατρική. In virtue, as elsewhere, it is the trained man who is the standard.

It is to be noticed that in the passage translated in the last paragraph, *Eth. Nic.* 1138 b 21, λόγος alone is used as equivalent to ὀρθὸς λόγος. In 1107 a 1, Aristotle says, "Virtue is . . . . a mean defined by λόγος and as the wise man would define it." Here too λόγος is equivalent to ὀρθὸς λόγος.

[1] Cf. 1140 b 5 and 20.
[2] It is therefore on insufficient grounds that Burnet, following Bywater, brackets the words in 1103 b 32, ῥηθήσεται δ' ὕστερον περὶ αὐτῶν καὶ τί ἐστιν ὁ ὀρθὸς λόγος καὶ πῶς ἔχει πρὸς τὰς ἄλλας ἀρετάς, on the ground that they imply the identification of the ὀρθὸς λόγος with φρόνησις, "which in this bald form is post-Aristotelian."

THE INTERMEDIARY POWERS 33

The affinity between ὁ ὀρθὸς λόγος in Aristotle and Plato's Idea of Good is obvious. ὁ ὀρθὸς λόγος is the Platonic Idea of Good restricted to the ethical sphere and with the mystic, metaphysical, and poetical elements excluded. The phrase σκοπὸς πρὸς ὃν ἀποβλέπων, *Eth. Nic.* 1138 b 22, suggests the Platonic ideas.[1] ὁ ὀρθὸς λόγος is the ideal in the mind of the man who is virtuous and whose virtue is not merely a matter of habit but is based on a true comprehension of the chief end of man and the relation of his concrete activities to it.[2]

In *Met.* 6:15, Aristotle uses λόγος in a way which suggests the ideas of Plato. ἐπεὶ δ' ἡ οὐσία ἑτέρα τό τε σύνολον καὶ ὁ λόγος (λέγω ὅτι ἡ μὲν οὕτως ἐστὶν οὐσία σὺν τῇ ὕλῃ συνειλημμένος ὁ λόγος, ἡ δ' ὁ λόγος ὅλως), ὅσαι μὲν οὖν οὕτω λέγονται, τούτων μὲν ἔστι φθορά· καὶ γὰρ γένεσις· τοῦ δὲ λόγου οὐκ ἔστιν οὕτως ὥστε φθείρεσθαι. λόγος here is the same as ἡ ἰδέα of chapter xiv of this book of the *Metaphysics* and of Plato with the notion of independent existence, of hypostatization, gone.[3] λόγος is also used by Aristotle as the equivalent of τὸ τί ἦν εἶναι, and εἶδος, expressions which are Aristotelian equivalents for the ideas of Plato.[4]

In the Stoic system, the word λόγος is enriched with these suggestions of the Platonic ideas. ὁ ὀρθὸς λόγος is for them, in one of its aspects, merely the power of reasonable thought, or the normal thought.[5] As such, it is the criterion which is the test of truth.[6] In the sphere of ethics, this normal thought is, as it is for Aristotle, the governing principle of the virtuous or happy life.[7] Now for the Stoics happiness consists in such a life as will lead to the fullest development of the nature of the individual. Such a life can only be that which is in harmony with the movement and law of the universe. In the case of a conscious,

[1] Cf. *Crat.* 389 A B; *Rep.* 484 C D; 500 B–D, 501 B; *Gorg.* 503 E. Compare the figurative expressions (τοῖ βλέπων, etc.) constantly used in Plato's *Laws* in connection with the recurrent theme of the ethical aim (σκοπός) of the lawgiver; *Laws* 625 E, 626 A, 630 C, 688 A, B, 693 B, 707 D, 714 B, 743 C, 757 C, 770 C, 962 A, D, 965 B, *et al.*

[2] "Keine allgemeine, objective Norm, sondern die φρόνησις in jedem einzelnen Menschen, welche die richtige Mitte bestimmt und auf welche demnach alle menschlichen Tugenden zurückzuführen sind." Heinze, *Lehre v. Logos*, p. 76.

[3] Cf. λόγοι ἔνυλοι, *De an.* i. 403 a 25.

[4] See Heinze, *op. cit.*, pp. 77 f.

[5] Animus rectus, bonus, magnus. Seneca *Epist.* 31:11.

[6] Bonhöffer, *Epictetus u.d. Stoa* (Stuttgart, 1890), I, 223; Heinze, *op. cit.*, p. 150; Diog. Laert. vii. 54.

[7] λόγος ὀρθὸς . . . . προστατικὸς μὲν τῶν ποιητέων, ἀπαγορευτικὸς δὲ τῶν οὐ ποιητέων. Stob. *Ecl.* ii. 190, 204. Cf. Heinze, *op. cit.*, p. 151, n. 3.

reasoning being, the complete life must be based on the knowledge of the universal law.[1] ὁ ὀρθὸς λόγος, the principle of the virtuous life, is, for the Stoics, identical with the λόγος which governs the changing world of matter. It is not surprising to find that in this sense the Stoics tend to hypostatize the notion. Diogenes Laertius (vii. 88), speaks of ὁ νόμος ὁ κοινὸς ὅσπερ ἐστὶν ὁ ὀρθὸς λόγος διὰ πάντων ἐρχόμενος ὁ αὐτὸς ὢν τῷ Διί.

The Logos of the Stoics occupies the place in their system which the Idea of Good does in that of Plato. It is at once a logical[2] and an ethical ἀρχή[3] and an explanation of things and events in the universe.[4] It is embodied in the universe and only as we consciously embody it in our own lives do we human beings attain that health and harmony of the soul which constitutes happiness.[5] This Reason differs from the Platonic Idea of Good in that it is identified with God[6] and in that it is material. The Stoics were monists and they did away with the opposition between matter and thought by boldly declaring that nothing existed which had no corporeal form.[7] The Logos is, for them, the fiery mind of the universe.[8]

Philo's doctrine differs from that of the Stoics in just these two conceptions. In the first place, the Logos does not, according to his teaching, exhaust the divine nature. It has already become evident above that the Logos is God's thought in its aspect as creative, or in so far as this can be manifested in material forms. It is, then, the revelation of God in so far as this can be made in the world of becoming, the activity of God so far as this can display itself in the universe, the supreme idea that can be grasped by finite minds. As such, it is "the God of us who are imperfect"[9] and terms and metaphors are applied to this revelation which are also applied to the Supreme Being. It is wrong to press the formal contradiction of *Leg. all.* 2:86, τὸ δὲ γενικώτατόν ἐστιν ὁ θεός, καὶ

[1] Diog. Laert. vii. 88; Epict. *Dis.* i. 6; M. Aurel. iii. 1.

[2] As in Plato we trace things back to one supreme idea, so in the Stoics we trace the λόγοι σπερματικοί back to the supreme λόγος. See Heinze, *op. cit.*, p. 120, on the mixture of the σπερματικοὶ λόγοι. The λόγος is the ἀρχή in physics and in ethics and so in all dialectics, just as the Idea of Good is in Plato. Discussion for the Stoics is settled when one discovers what is the λόγος, the reason of a thing.

[3] Cf. *supra*, note 2.

[4] Diog. Laert. vii. 134-36; Seneca *Epist.* 65:2; Heinze, *op. cit.*, pp. 125-28.

[5] See above, Diog. Laert. vii. 88. [6] Diog. Laert. vii. 88; Heinze, *op. cit.*, p. 85.

[7] Heinze, *op. cit.*, pp. 88 f.

[8] νοῦν κόσμου πύρινον; Zeno in Diels, *Dox. Gr.*, p. 303², l. 11.

[9] *Leg. all.* 3:207.

δεύτερος ὁ θεοῦ λόγος, and such passages as *Quod det. pot.* 118, τὸν πρεσβύτατον τῶν ὄντων λόγον θεῖον ὃς ὀνομάζεται τὸ γενικώτατον.[1] Usually τὸν γενικώτατον, when applied to the Logos, has some limiting phrase. In *Leg. all.* 3:175, for example, while the Logos is by inference said to be τὸ γενικώτατον τῶν ὄντων, Philo immediately adds καὶ ὁ λόγος δὲ τοῦ θεοῦ ὑπεράνω παντός ἐστι τοῦ κόσμου καὶ πρεσβύτατος καὶ γενικώτατος τῶν ὅσα γέγονε, where the phrase τῶν ὅσα γέγονε clearly distinguishes the Logos from the Supreme Being.[2] Again, it is no contradiction if at times activities are in some passages assigned to God and in others to the Logos. The Logos does not act of its own will. In *Conf. ling.* 175 we are told that the subordinate powers cannot act independently.[3] Strictly speaking, it is always God who acts through the Logos or through the powers.[4]

The second main difference between the Logos in Philo and in the Stoics is that in Philo the Logos is not material. Two passages have been used to show that at times Stoic materialism is to be found in Philo.[5] These illustrate Philo's use of Stoic terms in a sense which is manifestly not Stoic. The first passage is *De cherub.* 30. It is a part of an explanation of the flaming sword with which the cherubim guarded the way to the tree of life (Gen. 3:24). This sword represents the Logos. In § 28 we find the words ὀξυκινητότατον γὰρ καὶ θερμὸν λόγος καὶ μάλιστα ὁ τοῦ αἰτίου, ὅτι καὶ αὐτὸ πάντα φθάσαν παρημείψατο καὶ πρὸ πάντων νοούμενον καὶ ἐπὶ πᾶσι φαινόμενον. Again in § 30 he says φλογίνη δὲ ῥομφαία διότι χρὴ τούτοις (that is God's goodness and kingly power) παρακολουθεῖν τὸν μέσον τῶν πραγμάτων ἔνθερμον καὶ πυρώδη λόγον ὃς οὐδέποτε λήγει κινούμενος σπουδῇ πάσῃ πρὸς αἵρεσιν μὲν τῶν καλῶν, φυγὴν δὲ τῶν ἐναντίων. It is true that the phrase ἔνθερμον καὶ πυρώδη λόγον suggests Zeno's description of the νοῦν κόσμου as πύρινον. See Aet. Plac., i, 7, 23, in Diels, *Dox. Gr.*, p. 303², l. 11. But in this passage the word λόγος means "the thought power of God" and is not personified as a separate existence

[1] Bréhier, *Id. phil. et relig.*, p. 98.

[2] *Ibid.*, p. 98, n. 1, fails to notice this limiting phrase when he cites the passage as contradictory of *Leg. all.* 2:86. See further, for the difference between the Logos and God, Soulier, *Doctrine du Logos chez Philon* (Turin, 1876), pp. 98–105. God is older than the archetype of light, i.e., the Logos—*Somn.* 1:75; the Logos is his εἰκων—*Conf. ling.* 97; the ἀσκητής can attain to the Logos, the αὐτομαθής to God himself—*Somn.* 1:68–71. For a distinction similar to that between the Logos and the Supreme Being see pseudo-Platonic *Ep.* VI. 323 C and Shorey's note in *Class. Phil.*, X, 88.

[3] Drummond, *op. cit.*, II, 70 f.

[4] Cf. *De cherub.* 127; *Leg. all.* 3:96; *Mig. Ab.* 6; Drummond, *op. cit.*, II, 70 f.

[5] Bréhier, *op. cit.*, p. 85.

from God. It is His reason, that of which the human reason is the imitation (§ 31). In this passage λόγος θεοῦ is equivalent to ὀρθὸς λόγος. It is by His λόγος that God is ruler and that He is good (§ 28). This λόγος is that which unceasingly chooses the good and shuns the evil (§ 30). Moreover Philo makes it plain that he is using the terms ὀξυκινητότατον and θερμόν in a metaphorical sense. In § 28 he explains the words as meaning that λόγος, here equivalent to "thought" in general, is the swiftest of all things and is grasped by our senses in all things. So in § 30 the λόγος is ἔνθερμον καὶ πυρῶδη "because of its continued motion with all zeal to choose the fair and avoid the base." This does not admit of a materialistic interpretation.

A second passage interpreted by some[1] as implying materialism is *Quis rer. div.* 79. Philo is here explaining the name Israel which, he says, is equivalent to ὁ ὁρῶν. ὁ μὲν γὰρ ἀνατείνει τὰς ὄψεις πρὸς αἰθέρα καὶ τὰς οὐρανοῦ περιόδους, πεπαίδευται δὲ καὶ εἰς τὸ μάννα ἀφορᾶν, τὸν θεῖον λόγον, τὴν οὐράνιον ψυχῆς φιλοθεάμονος ἄφθαρτον τροφήν. The quotation of the entire passage is sufficient to show that there is no materialism. The Greek does not imply so close a parallelism as Bréhier seems to think it does between the Logos and the revolutions of the heaven. Notice the καὶ before εἰς τὸ μάννα. The word ἀφορᾶν suggests the Platonic ideas.[2] The term τροφή is used of wisdom and the ideas in both Philo and Plato.[3]

It is true that the Logos is described by Philo, in language reminiscent of the Stoic ἕξις, as the glue and bond,[4] as the unbreakable bond of the universe[5] and as extended through all things,[6] filling all things with its essence;[7] but this does not mean that Philo's thought is here materialistic.[8] Plato's language in *Phaedo* 99 C, τὸ ἀγαθὸν καὶ δέον συνδεῖν καὶ συνέχειν, does not imply materialism, neither does the description of Eros in *Symp.* 203 A as that which binds the universe together. We have already dealt in the chapter on "The Ultimate Reality" with such expressions as πάντα τῆς οὐσίας ἐκπεπληρωκώς in *Quis rer. div.* 188 (pp. 15 f. above). It is impossible to avoid the metaphorical use of materialistic

---

[1] Bréhier, *loc. cit.*

[2] Cf. *Crat.* 389 A, D; *Phaedo* 99 E; *Rep.* 484 C, 500 D; *Gorg.* 503 D E. See Shorey, *Idea of Good in Plato's Republic*, p. 226.

[3] Cf. *Phaedr.* 247 C D; *Quis rer. div.* 191; *Leg. all.* 1:97.

[4] *Quis rer. div.* 188.

[5] *De plant.* 9; cf. *V.M.* 2:133; *Somn.* 1:241.

[6] *Quis rer. div.* 217.   [7] *Quis rer. div.* 188. Cf. διοικοῦντος in *V.M.* 2:133.

[8] Bréhier, *op. cit.*, p. 85.

language in order to represent the relation of the idea to its material embodiment. It is wrong to press such metaphors and make Philo abandon what is so basic in his doctrine as the dualistic separation between matter and thought.

Philo's doctrine differs from that of the Stoics, then, in these two ways; he rejects their materialism and their identification of the Logos with the Supreme Being. It is in these two aspects and only in these that the Stoic Logos differs from the Platonic Idea of Good. In spite, then, of the fact that Philo adopts almost in its entirety the language of Stoicism in regard to the Logos,[1] his teaching is Platonic. He uses the current word of his day and speaks of the reason or reasonableness of God rather than His goodness, no doubt partly from apologetic motives but probably also because, for him, the word "goodness" tended to mean "graciousness." God's reasonableness is manifested in His δύναμις βασιλική or δύναμις κολαστική, as well as in His goodness, or δύναμις χαριστική.[2] There is a stern side to Philo's God. Both the sternness and the graciousness are, however, reasonable and good.

It seems clear, then, that Philo's Reason or Reasonableness is not essentially different from Plato's Good. It is the ἀρχή, the final standard in all dialectic. Human thought can see the reason in things, or, to use another Stoic expression which is equivalent and based on Plato, can see the πρόνοια of God manifested in the world.[3] Back of this we cannot go. All thought, all existence, all conduct, must, in order to be finally valid, be based on this ἀρχή. It is at once the law of nature and an ideal to which man must conform his life. Now the visible universe is a perfect being so that in it ὀρθὸς λόγος is completely embodied. From the point of view of man, it makes no difference whether we think of this ideal as embodied in the universe or as existing in transcendence. Hence in Philo ὀρθὸς λόγος is at times spoken of as a copy of the divine Logos and sometimes as itself the divine Logos.[4] The difference between the

---

[1] Heinze, *op. cit.*, pp. 235-45; Bréhier, *op. cit.*, p. 85.

[2] *Quis rer. div.* 166; *Sp. leg.* 1:307; *Quaes. in Gen.* 1:57; *V.M.* 2:99; *De Ab.* 124.

[3] *De aet. m.* 37. See Heinze, *op. cit.*, p. 127, and compare Stob. *Ecl.* i. 178 and Plato *Laws* 898 E. Cf. Shorey's article on "Greek Philosophy," Hastings' *Encyc. of Relig. and Ethics*, IX, 861-62.

[4] Cf. Bréhier, *op. cit.*, p. 95. For the latter see *De ag.* 51, τὸν ὀρθὸν λόγον αὐτοῦ καὶ πρωτόγονον υἱόν. λόγος is often the equivalent of νόμος. Cf. *V.M.* 2:52 where τῷ λόγῳ τῆς ἀιδίου φύσεως is equivalent to νόμῳ φύσεως. Also *Somn.* 2:223, 237; *Jos.* 174; *Conf. ling.* 41-43. The λόγος is the ἀρχὴ καὶ πηγή of all the virtues in *De post. C.* 127; the πηγὴ σοφίας in *Fug. et Inv.* 97. Cf. *Fug. et Inv.* 137. In *De gig.* 17 the sciences and virtues are daughters of ὀρθὸς λόγος.

Logos embodied in the world and as transcendent idea is a difference in the clearness and consistency of the idea rather than in its actual content. The Logos is the law of the visible universe.[1]

While there is this emphasis on the moral aspects of the Logos, we must beware of thinking of it as composed of moral beings and ideal virtues only. It contains the ideas of sensation and of sensible things[2] as well as of mind and of the virtues. In Philo, as in Plato, the emphasis is, naturally, on the high moral concepts, but in both thinkers the ideas are counterparts of things, as well as of moral dispositions.[3]

In *De op. mund.* 25, the Logos seems to be the model according to which visible human beings were formed. Here the Logos would naturally be regarded as the idea of the composite being formed of soul and body. But *De op. mund.* 69 shows that we are not to interpret the passage in this sense. So in *De op. mund.* 139, the Logos is the model for the soul only and it is in this sense that the Logos may be regarded as the idea of man. It is the idea of man in the feature that distinguishes him from the animals, the distinctively human element in us.[4]

The Logos as ideal man is called ὁ κατ' εἰκόνα ἄνθρωπος, where κατ' εἰκόνα is to be interpreted as the equivalent of εἰκών.[5] Sometimes it is called ἄνθρωπος ἀσώματος.[6] Again, owing to the ambiguity of the expression, the individual man or rather the human intelligence is called ὁ κατ' εἰκόνα ἄνθρωπος.[7] Heinze[8] and Bréhier[9] think that Philo

[1] Cf. Bréhier, *op. cit.*, p. 100; *Mig. Ab.* 130. See also *De eb.* 34.

[2] See *Leg. all.* 1:22-24; *Sp. leg.* 1:45-49.

[3] Philo *De op. mund.* 18-20; 129-30; Plato *Crat.* 389 A B; *Rep.* 596 A B, 597 B.

[4] Drummond, *Phil. Jud.*, II, 275 f., agrees with the view here stated, but bases his conclusion on the consideration that the Logos could not include the idea of perception. This is a mistake. See *Sp. leg.* 1:45-49; *Leg. all.* 1:22-24.

[5] *Conf. ling.* 146. Note that the Logos is called ὁ κατ' εἰκόνα ἄνθρωπος and then later (§ 147) εἰκών. Cf. *De plant.* 44.

[6] *Conf. ling.* 62 f.

[7] *De op. mund.* 25 where ὁ κατ' εἰκόνα is equivalent to εἰκων εἰκόνος. See *De op. mund.* 69; cf. 134; *Leg. all.* 3:96, 2:4. The expression emphasizes man's dignity as an earthly image of God. Cf. *Quaes. in Gen.* 1:93, "coelestis ille homo." In contrast with the idea of mind, οὐράνιος νοῦς, the concrete human νοῦς, until it receives the πνεῦμα of God, is earthly and mortal. See *Leg. all.* 1:31-32. Once Philo speaks of it as ὁ αἰσθητὸς λόγος, *Leg. all.* 3:179.

[8] *Lehre v. Logos*, pp. 260 f.

[9] *Id. phil. et relig.*, p. 122. Bréhier refers to *Leg. all.* 3:96. But there is no reference there to the *ideal* man. The passage reads ὡς τῆς μὲν εἰκόνος (i.e., εἰκόνος θεοῦ) κατὰ τὸν θεὸν ἀπεικονισθείσης, τοῦ δὲ ἀνθρώπου κατὰ τὴν εἰκόνα λαβούσαν δύναμιν παραδείγματος. The κατὰ τὴν εἰκόνα is of course not attributive.

does not identify the Logos with the man made in the image, or the heavenly man. The identification is clear in *Conf. ling.* 62, where the ideal man (ἀσώματον) is said to "differ not at all from the divine image. Him the Father of the universe caused to rise as the oldest son, whom elsewhere he has called the first-born, who, when begotten, imitating the ways of his Father[1] looking to archetypal patterns, moulded the species." Here ἀδιαφοροῦντα εἰκόνος would not be decisive in itself, but when found in connection with such expressions for the Logos as πρεσβύτατον υἱόν,[2] πρωτόγονον,[3] ἐμόρφου τὰ εἴδη[4] there can be no reasonable doubt that the Logos is meant.

The ideal man is not, however, consistently identified with the Logos. In *De op. mund.* 134, the ideal man is contrasted with the earthly, composite man, but in § 139 the Logos is mentioned as the archetype of the soul only. How little Philo cares for consistency in the whole mythology of the ideal man is shown by the fact[5] that he specifically refers in *De op. mund.* 134 to his account of the man κατ' εἰκόνα in § 69 of the same treatise, but gives a totally different interpretation of the phrase. In § 69, the man made in the image is the mind or soul of man; in § 134, it is the ideal man of which individuals are copies. A further inconsistency is that in *De op. mund.* 134, the idea of man is "neither male nor female," while in *Leg. all.* 2:13 it is said to include these two species. At times the Logos is itself the idea of man[6] or the idea of intelligence.[7] At other times the idea of man[8] or the idea of intelligence[9] apparently comes in between the individual man and the Logos.

In view of this indifference to consistency, Bréhier is wrong in finding in the variation of the interpretation of ὁ κατ' εἰκόνα ἄνθρωπος support for his theory that the *De op. mund.* and the *Allegories* belong to different series of treatises.[10] Nor can the variety in the interpretation of Adam be regarded as a sure basis for such a conclusion. It is true that in *De op. mund.* 135-40, Adam is pictured mythically as the perfect man, surpassing in power and in intelligence all his descendants, while in the *Allegories*, 1:31 ff., he is the mind which enters into matter and appears

---

[1] Cf. μιμούμενοι τὸν σφέτερον δημιουργόν, *Tim.* 42 E.

[2] *Quod det. pot.* 118.   [3] *De ag.* 51.

[4] Cf. *Leg. all.* 1:21. τὰ εἴδη does not mean the ideas as Bréhier (*Id. phil.*, p. 126, n. 1) seems to interpret it. Note πρὸς τὰ παραδείγματα βλέπων.

[5] Pointed out by Bréhier, *op. cit.*, p. 121.

[6] *De op. mund.* 25.   [8] *Ibid.* 134.

[7] *Ibid.* 69.   [9] *Leg. all.* 1:31-32.

[10] Bréhier, *op. cit.*, p. 123; cf. p. 92, n. 2.

to have given up to the ideal man, here the heavenly archetype of the human intelligence, all the superiorities that were his in the *De op. mund.* But in the passage from the *Allegories*, Adam is contrasted, not with subsequent generations of men, but with the heavenly archetype of the human mind. The "caelestis homo" of *Quaes. in Gen.* 1:93 is not the same as the man made in the image of God who is described in the *De op. mund.* He is simply man as distinguished from the animals. Note "mixtura conflata ex anima et corpore" and compare for the use of "caelestis" in this connection οὐράνιον φυτόν in *Quod det. pot.* 85, Frg. in M. 647, *De plant.* 17. See also οὐράνιον φυτόν in Plato *Timaeus* 90 A.

In the mythology of the Logos, Philo has been influenced by several Platonic sources. The description of Eros in *Symp.* 202 D f. supplies many phrases that are used by Philo to describe the Logos in his function as mediator between God and man. A citation of parallels is sufficient to show the Platonic influence.

Plato	Philo
Symp. 202 D: μεταξὺ θνητοῦ καὶ ἀθανάτου. Μεταξὺ . . . . θεοῦ τε καὶ θνητοῦ.	*Quis rer. div.* 205: ἵνα μεθόριος στὰς τὸ γενόμενον διακρίνῃ τοῦ πεποιηκότος.
Symp. 202 E: ἐν μέσῳ δὲ ὂν ἀμφοτέρων.	*Ibid.* 206: οὔτε ἀγένητος ὡς ὁ θεὸς ὢν οὔτε γενητὸς ὡς ὑμεῖς, ἀλλὰ μέσος τῶν ἄκρων.
Symp. 202 E: ἑρμηνεῦον καὶ διαπορθμεῦον θεοῖς τὰ παρ' ἀνθρώπων καὶ ἀνθρώποις τὰ παρὰ θεῶν, τῶν μὲν τὰς δεήσεις καὶ θυσίας, τῶν δὲ τὰς ἐπιτάξεις τε καὶ ἀμοιβὰς τῶν θυσιῶν.[1]	*Leg. all.* 3:207: τοῦ ἑρμηνέως λόγου.
	Quis rer. div. 205: ἱκέτης μὲν ἐστι τοῦ θνητοῦ κηραίνοντος ἀεὶ πρὸς τὸ ἄφθαρτον, πρεσβευτὴς δὲ τοῦ ἡγεμόνος πρὸς τὸ ὑπήκοον.
	Somn. 1:141: ταύτας δαίμονας μὲν οἱ ἄλλοι φιλόσοφοι, ὁ δὲ ἱερὸς λόγος ἀγγέλους εἴωθε καλεῖν . . . . τὰς τοῦ πατρὸς ἐπικελεύσεις τοῖς ἐγγόνοις καὶ τὰς τῶν ἐγγόνων χρείας τῷ πατρὶ διαγγέλλουσι.
	De gig. 12: πρὸς τὴν τῶν θνητῶν ἐπιστασίαν.

[1] It is on the passage from the *Symp.* here quoted that the doctrine of the Logos as High Priest is based. See *Somn.* 1:215, *Somn.* 2:183, 185-89.

THE INTERMEDIARY POWERS 41

PLATO	PHILO
Symp. 202 E: συμπληροῖ, ὥστε τὸ πᾶν αὐτὸ αὑτῷ συνδεδέσθαι.	*Quis rer. div.* 188: κόλλα γὰρ καὶ δεσμὸς οὗτος πάντα τῆς οὐσίας ἐκπεπληρωκώς.
Cf. *Phaedo* 99 C: τὸ ἀγαθὸν καὶ δέον συνδεῖν καὶ συνέχειν.	*Fug. et Inv.* 112: δεσμὸς ὢν τῶν ἁπάντων, ὡς εἴρηται, καὶ συνέχει τὰ μέρη πάντα καὶ σφίγγει, κωλύων αὐτὰ διαλύεσθαι καὶ διαρτᾶσθαι.
Symp. 203 A: θεὸς δὲ ἀνθρώπῳ οὐ μείγνυται, ἀλλὰ διὰ τούτου πᾶσά ἐστιν ἡ ὁμιλία καὶ ἡ διάλεκτος θεοῖς πρὸς ἀνθρώπους καὶ ἐγρηγορόσι καὶ καθεύδουσι.	*Somn.* 1:69: οὐ γὰρ ἀξιῶν ὁ θεὸς εἰς αἴσθησιν ἔρχεσθαι τοὺς ἑαυτοῦ λόγους ἐπικουρίας ἕνεκα τῶν φιλαρέτων ἀποστέλλει.
	Somn. 1:190: ὀνείρους . . . . οὐ μόνον τοὺς κατὰ τὸ πρεσβύτατον τῶν αἰτίων προφαινομένους, ἀλλὰ καὶ τοὺς διὰ τῶν ὑποφητῶν αὐτοῦ καὶ ὀπαδῶν ἀγγέλων.

A second Platonic source is the doctrine of the younger gods in the *Timaeus*.[1] This passage suggests the part which the Logoi play as creators of man in Philo. The reason given for the assignment of man's creation to subordinate beings is the same in Philo and in Plato. God cannot be responsible for evil. Man, with his nature prone to sin, must be created by some subordinate power.

A third Platonic source is the myth of the *Phaedrus*. In the *Symposium*, Plato had spoken of "the tribe of demons which, being in the midst betwixt these twain—the Godhead and Mankind—filleth up that distance."[2] In the *Phaedrus* (247 A f.) Plato speaks as if he thought of souls dwelling in the air. It was easy to identify these souls with the demons of the myth of the *Symposium*. This is what Philo does. There are two main passages for the doctrine. The one that best suits our present purpose is *De gig.* 6–18.[3]

---

[1] *Tim.* 41 A–42 E. Note especially 42 D, ἵνα τῆς ἔπειτα εἴη κακίας ἑκάστων ἀναίτιος. Cf. *Conf. ling.* 176–79. So these "powers," according to Philo, punish men, since God should not be the cause of things that even seem to be evil. *Conf. ling.* 181; cf. ibid. 171; *Decal.* 178.

[2] *Symp.* 202 E. Translation by Stewart, *Myths of Plato*, p. 415.

[3] The ideas are repeated in *Somn.* 1:134–43.

What other philosophers call demons Moses was accustomed to call angels. They are souls that flit about in the air. . . . . Of these souls [§ 12], some descended into bodies, others demanded that they be not conformed to any of the parts of earth. These, being sanctified and embracing the service of the Father, the Creator is wont to use as His servants and ministers for the government of mortals. The others, after descending into the body as into a river, at times are seized and drawn down as by the suction of a most violent whirlpool, at times again through their ability to resist the current they at first swim up, then soar aloft to the place from whence they came. These are the souls of the genuine philosophers that from beginning to end practise to die to the bodily life that they may gain a share of the life that is incorruptible and free of the body, the life that is with the unbegotten and incorruptible.

The explanation of the rise and fall of the soul is in striking accord with the *Phaedrus*, though the figure of the river, which determines so much of the phraseology, comes from the *Timaeus*. In the *Phaedrus*, of those souls which are not able to rise above the air, "some, filled with forgetfulness and wickedness, and made heavy, shed the feathers of their wings and fall unto the earth." These are planted in the bodies of men or beasts. The soul which, in its life in the air, saw most of the divine things "passes into the seed of a man who shall become a seeker after the True Wisdom, a Seeker after the True Beauty, a Friend of the Muses, a True Lover" (248 C D, Stewart's translation). Such a man "getteth wings and desireth with them to fly up, but is not able."

The number of Platonic reminiscences in the passage in Philo indicates that he is here in conscious dependence on Plato. It is worth while to exhibit these in detail.

Plato	Philo
Phaedo 67 E: οἱ ὀρθῶς φιλοσοφοῦντες ἀποθνήσκειν μελετῶσι.	*De gig.* 14: αὗται μὲν οὖν εἰσι ψυχαὶ τῶν ἀνόθως φιλοσοφησάντων, ἐξ ἀρχῆς ἄχρι τέλους μελετῶσαι τὸν μετὰ σωμάτων ἀποθνήσκειν βίον.
Symp. 202 E: Ἑρμηνεῦον καὶ διαπορθμεῦον θεοῖς τὰ παρ' ἀνθρώπων καὶ ἀνθρώποις τὰ παρὰ θεῶν.	*De gig.* 16: πρεσβευτάς τινας ἀνθρώπων πρὸς θεὸν καὶ θεοῦ πρὸς ἀνθρώπους.
Phaedr. 249 D: πτερῶταί τε καὶ ἀναπτερούμενος προθυμούμενος ἀνάπτεσθαι.	*De gig.* 13: ἐκεῖσε πάλιν ἀνέπτησαν.

THE INTERMEDIARY POWERS 43

Plato	Philo
Phaedr. 250 E: ἐκεῖσε φέρεται.	
Phaedr. 250 C: καθαροὶ ὄντες καὶ ἀσήμαντοι τούτου ὃ νῦν σῶμα περιφέροντες ὀνομάζομεν.	*De gig.* 14: ἵνα τῆς ἀσωμάτου καὶ ἀφθάρτου παρὰ τῷ ἀγενήτῳ καὶ ἀφθάρτῳ ζωῆς μεταλάχωσιν.
Symp. 210 E: κατόψεταί τι θαυμαστὸν . . . . πρῶτον μὲν ἀεὶ ὂν καὶ οὔτε γιγνόμενον οὔτε ἀπολλύμενον.	
Tim. 42 E: τοῦτο καὶ πάντα ὅσα ἀκόλουθα ἐκείνοις ἀπεργασαμένους ἄρχειν καὶ . . . . τὸ θνητὸν διακυβερνᾶν ζῷον.	*De gig.* 12: πρὸς τὴν τῶν θνητῶν ἐπιστασίαν.
Tim. 43 A: ἐνέδουν εἰς ἐπίρρυτον σῶμα καὶ ἀπόρρυτον. αἱ δ' εἰς ποταμὸν ἐνδεθεῖσαι.	*De gig.* 13: ἐκεῖναι δ' ὥσπερ εἰς ποταμὸν τὸ σῶμα καταβᾶσαι, etc. The figure is carried out all through the section.

Philo explains that evil demons are merely souls who have taken up their abode in bodies. The good demons are the creative and governing spirits called younger gods in the *Timaeus* and demons in the *Symposium*.

Philo's proofs for the existence of spirits in the air (*De gig.* 6–12), at first sight suggest that he, for the moment at least, regards the soul as composed of air. The proofs are, first, that since all other elements have living beings in them, it is reasonable to suppose that the air is no exception. Second, it is the air that nourishes the land and water animals. When foul it causes plagues, when pure it makes these creatures stronger. It is therefore likely that, even if the other elements were barren of living creatures, μόνος ἀὴρ ὤφειλε ζῳοτοκῆσαι τὰ ψυχῆς κατ' ἐξαιρετὸν χάριν παρὰ τοῦ δημιουργοῦ σπέρματα λαβών. The language here is certainly Stoic. Compare Arnim, *Frg.*, II, 303, number 1014. If we press the word ζῳοτοκῆσαι, the materialistic interpretation is inevitable. But where language is as highly colored as Philo's is, we must not press such a word, particularly in a mythical passage such as this. There is no reason to suppose that Philo is here doing more than support the myth by an *argumentum ad hominem*.

That Philo has been greatly influenced in his doctrine of the intermediary powers by writers other than Plato there can be no doubt.

The pseudo-Platonic *Epinomis*[1] has contributed suggestions. A nearer parallel is to be found in Posidonius' elaborate theory of intermediaries.[2] It is probable that the doctrine was a part of the general belief of the time.[3] But the doctrine is a natural development of Platonism. In any estimate we may make of Philo, it is necessary to remember that this particular doctrine is a consciously mythological and metaphorical description of the activity of God.

As phases of the divine activity, or thoughts of God, the powers share His transcendence of human thought. In *Sp. leg.* 1:47, it is said that in their essence they cannot be comprehended. So in *Quod Deus sit* 77, God uses His powers unmixed, but when they have to do with the world of becoming they are weakened. Otherwise, our human weakness could not bear their splendor. Here Philo is speaking of God's "knowledge, wisdom, prudence, justice, and other virtues" (§ 79). In the passage cited from *Sp. leg.* 1:47, the powers are not only God's virtues, but His creative activities, more especially the ideas.[4] These incorporeal natures, contrasted with "lifeless opinions," are called timeless.[5] Such exaltation leads directly toward personification of the powers in the imagination as subordinate gods.[6]

Philo makes large use of Stoic vocabulary[7] throughout this part of his teaching, but the difference between his conception and that of the Stoics is that he regards these Logoi as thoughts of God and so as incorporeal laws of being, while the Stoics think of them as material air currents.[8] Here as elsewhere we must remember that the use of metaphors from the material sphere does not necessarily imply materialism. Philo's constant emphasis on the incorporeality of the Logoi, his identification of them with the ideas, ought to be accepted as proof that he did not at any time seriously adopt the Stoic materialism.

[1] Cf. *Epinomis* 981 C D, 982 A–984 B with *De gig.* 6 ff., *Somn.* 1:134 f. and see Bréhier, *Id. phil.*, pp. 128 f.

[2] See M. Apelt, *De rationibus quibusdam quae Philoni cum Posidonio intercedunt*, pp. 103–9.

[3] See Bevan, *Stoics and Skeptics* (Oxford, 1913), p. 95.

[4] Note παραφαίνουσιν ἐκμαγεῖόν τι καὶ ἀπεικόνισμα τῆς ἑαυτῶν ἐνεργείας, and the image of the seal and wax.

[5] *De sac. A. et C.* 69. Cf. ἀπερίγραφοι of the powers in *De sac. A. et C.* 59, ἀπερίγραφοι καὶ ἀτελεύτητοι of the χάριτες of God in *De op. mund.* 23. In *Mut. nom.* 15 the Logos is described as κυρίῳ ὀνόματι οὐ ῥητὸς ῥημῖν.

[6] They are prayed to in *De plant.* 46. Cf. *Fug. et Inv.* 212.

[7] See Zeller, *Phil. der Griech.*, Vol. III, Part II, p. 390.

[8] See Zeller, *Stoics, Epicureans, and Skeptics*, pp. 127–31.

THE INTERMEDIARY POWERS 45

These angels, demons, powers, or Logoi are grouped under two supreme Logoi, Goodness and Sovereignty.[1] These in turn are subordinate to the Divine Logos. The Logos is described as an angel in *De cherub.* 3 and 35, *Mut. nom.* 87, *Fug. et Inv.* 5, *Quod Deus sit* 182. He is the ἡνίοχος or ἔποχος of the powers (*Fug. et Inv.* 101). He is their father and guide (*Somn.* 2:185 ff.); the place which God fills with them (*Somn.* 1:62). He is the oldest of the angels, the archangel (*Conf. ling.* 146). In *Quaes. in Ex.* 2:68 (M., pp. 515 f.), there is a hierarchy of beings, God, the Logos, the creative and kingly powers, the beneficent and punishing powers, the intelligible world. In this passage God is "dicens" and the Logos is "verbum." The lack of consistency between the different classifications and groupings, shows that Philo did not take the matter seriously.

The identification of the Logos with the neo-Pythagorean unity or seven does not at all change the underlying conception. Philo finds Pythagorean mysticism, and consequently its vocabulary, congenial. Bréhier (*op. cit.*, pp. 107 ff.), shows interesting parallels between the Logos of Philo, the Hermes-Logos of Cornutus and the Osiris of Plutarch's "Isis and Osiris." The tendency to personify moral and physical conceptions was a characteristic which Philo shared with his contemporaries in Greek philosophy. The parallels which Bréhier adduces do not show that Philo is drawn aside from his adherence to Plato. He can readily adopt any terminology and any metaphors which suit his underlying conception of the Logos as at once the reason of God and the idea of the universe.

Philo's indifference to consistency in his mythology is shown by the rôle he assigns to the divine wisdom. Sometimes this seems to be merely another name for the Logos,[2] but in other passages it is expressly described as superior to the Logos[3] and in still others as subordinate.[4] There is no effort after consistency and Philo varies his account as the exigencies of the allegorical method demand. It is impossible to suppose that in such doctrines Philo is setting forth his serious philosophical creed. The ἱερὸς γάμος between God and wisdom; the description of

---

[1] *De cherub.* 27; *Sp. leg.* 1:307; *Fug. et Inv.* 95. By His goodness God is θεός, by his sovereignty κύριος. See *Quis rer. div.* 166; *V.M.* 2:99; *Somn.* 1:163; *De Ab.* 121; *Sp. leg.* 1:307. For the κολαστική (=βασιλική) alone see *Conf. ling.* 182, 187; the χαριστική alone, *Conf. ling.* 137; *Sp. leg.* 4:187; *De praem.* 122.

[2] As means of creation, *Fug. et Inv.* 109; *De eb.* 30. As principle of virtue, *Quaes. in Gen.* 1:118; *Fug. et Inv.* 52; *Leg. all.* 1:43, 64 f., 2:86. As divider, *Fug. et Inv.* 194–96.

[3] *Somn.* 2:242 f. [4] *Fug. et Inv.* 97.

Wisdom as now the wife of God and now the daughter; the characterization of Wisdom by terms used of Athene; all these are interesting as showing the probable sources of the metaphors which Philo uses,[1] but the parallels do not at all compel us to think of Philo as adopting these superstitions as his serious belief. His clear recognition of the metaphorical nature of the other beings is sufficient warrant for regarding him as equally free from superstition here.[2] The freedom with which terms are varied shows that Philo was not "en face de notions données et irréductibles"[3] but rather that the myth plays no real part in his serious thought.

[1] See Bréhier, *Id. phil. et relig.*, pp. 118 f.
[2] See above, p. 28, with note 5.   [3] Bréhier, *op. cit.*, p. 115.

CHAPTER IV.

MAN'S SOUL AND ITS POWERS

Philo's ethical convictions are the dominant influence in his psychology, as well as in his theory of reality. He is sure that virtue and happiness are somehow in accord, that man will find the fulfilment of his life, not in the indulgence of his senses, but in the activity of reason. His primary classification of the powers of the soul is the one which best accords with this conviction, the distinction, that is, between the pure reason and the faculties subordinate to reason and dependent on the body. With this main point guarded, Philo adopts from the theories current in his day such details as he finds useful. The exigencies of the allegorical method of interpretation lead him to adopt a widely varying terminology. The Stoic vocabulary, so largely current in his day, is adopted at times even where it seems to contradict the main article of his ethical creed. The foundation of his thought is, however, to be found in Platonism. His teaching on the divisions of the soul can be presented more easily after a brief statement of the views of those of his predecessors who most largely influenced him.

The main distinction on which Philo insists, that between the rational and the irrational soul, is the primary distinction in Plato. Apart from this, Plato adopts or invents such speculations as best suit his purpose in any particular dialogue.[1] The common tripartite division of the soul is reached by subdividing the irrational part into θυμός and ἐπιθυμία. This is clear in the myth of the *Phaedrus*, where reason is the charioteer and θυμός and ἐπιθυμία are the two horses.[2] Reason is in a different category from the other two. So in the *Timaeus* 69 C f., θυμός and ἐπιθυμία both belong to the mortal part of the soul. In *Laws* 863 D, θυμός is a πάθος. It shows how little Plato cared for formal consistency in such matters, that in the *Phaedrus*, θυμός and ἐπιθυμία are, if we press the figure, parts of the pre-existent, immortal soul, though the *Timaeus* regards them as belonging to the mortal part. Plato speaks of "parts" (μέρη) of the soul as though there were separate divisions of the soul

---

[1] Hicks, *Aristotle's De Anima* (Cambridge, 1907), p. xxix; Brett, *A History of Psychology, Ancient and Patristic* (London, 1912), pp. 66 and 68.

[2] *Phaedr.* 245 C–256 D, especially 246 A B.

corresponding to these different functions,[1] and he even locates these parts in different bodily organs. Thought has its dwelling in the head, courage in the breast, desire in the lower part.[2] He warns us, however, that the division is not to be taken as scientifically accurate and final.[3] He questions whether we do not act with the whole soul in performing each function.[4] Of these parts or functions of the soul, reason is peculiar to man, animals have courage,[5] plants have desire.[6] Where the higher part exists, the lower must be presupposed, but the converse is not true.[7]

Aristotle criticises Plato's tripartite or dual division of the soul on three grounds. His first ground of criticism is that, if the soul is capable of being divided, we have to look for some other incorporeal and indivisible συνέχον and we might as well let the soul itself serve (*De an.* i. 5. 411 *b* 5). In the second place, division of the soul is useless because if we are to divide it according to its functions we must make an infinite number of divisions (*De an.* iii. 9. 432 *a* 22 f.). In the third place, there are other functions that differ from one another more widely than do those which Plato has made the basis of his division. Aristotle suggests as more adequate the fivefold division into θρεπτικόν, αἰσθητικόν, νοητικόν, βουλευτικόν, ὀρεκτικόν. He does not seek to meet his own criticisms regarding the συνέχον.[8]

In his general attitude to the soul and its divisions, he does not differ from Plato in any important detail. The Platonic division of the soul into the rational and irrational parts is accepted as sufficiently accurate for the purposes of his popular treatment of ethics in *Eth. Nic.* 1102 *a* 26. He adopts a further division of the soul into nutritive, assigned to plants, sensitive, assigned to animals, and reasoning or thinking, assigned to man.[9] This division is, as has been shown above, suggested in Plato. As in *Rep.* 582 f., the higher presupposes the lower, but the reverse is not true. It is important for the origin of the Stoic theory to notice

---

[1] *Rep.* 442 C; 444 B.

[2] *Tim.* 69 E, 90 A. Brett, *op. cit.*, p. 69.

[3] *Tim.* 72 D; cf. *Phaedr.* 246 A.

[4] *Rep.* 436 A; cf. *Rep.* 612 A; *Phaedr.* 271 A. For Plato's lack of dogmatism in this connection, see Shorey, *Unity of Plato's Thought*, pp. 42 f., 44 f. and n. 312. Cf. *Rep.* 477 C. For a complete account of Plato's views see also Zeller, *Plato and the Older Academy*, pp. 413–19; Hicks, *Aristotle's De Anima*, pp. xxix–xxxv; Brett, *op. cit.*, pp. 65–99.

[5] *Rep.* 441 B.   [6] *Tim.* 77 B.   [7] *Rep.* 582 A ff.

[8] See Zeller, *Aristotle*, II, 23, n. 1.

[9] *De an.* ii. 2. 413 *b* 12; iii. 3. 415 *a* 1–10.

that the nutritive part includes the reproductive (*De an.* ii. 4. 416 *a* 19). Of these three divisions of the soul, reason, the form peculiar to man, is exalted so that it is set off as a class by itself. This part of the soul cannot be entangled in the life of the body. It is χωριστός while the other parts are ἀχώριστοι.[1] It is simple, changeless, impassible,[2] immortal and eternal,[3] a γένος ἕτερον.[4] The other parts of the soul form a group set over against it. Aristotle's position, then, is practically that of Plato.

For Plato and Aristotle the soul was not material. The Stoics regarded it as a substance, a πνεῦμα ἔνθερμον.[5] This warm breath was connected in primitive fashion with the blood.[6] The dominant part the Stoics located in the heart and from this as a center currents of warm air passed out into the various organs of sense.[7] The Stoics, accordingly, regarded the five senses as parts of the soul. Speech and reproduction, as activities of the dominant part, were included in the list of its divisions. They distinguished, therefore, eight parts, if we regard the ἡγεμονικόν as a part.[8] The ἡγεμονικόν is, however, active in each of these.[9] In the Stoic system we see again that the ἡγεμονικόν, also called διανοητικόν, λογιστικόν or λογισμός,[10] corresponds to λόγος in Plato and Aristotle and is set over against the other parts of the soul which collectively form the irrational part.[11] The distinction which was of chief importance for Plato is the prime one in their system.

Just as in the speculations of Plato and Aristotle, so in the Stoic system, man is distinguished from beings of a lower order by the possession of reason. The Stoics divided all things in nature into four classes,

[1] *Gen. an.* ii. 3. 736 *b*; *De an.* ii. 2. 413 *b* 24 f. τοῦτο μόνον ἐνδέχεται χωρίζεσθαι καθάπερ τὸ ἀΐδιον τοῦ φθαρτοῦ.

[2] Simple, *De an.* iii. 4. 429 *a* 18; cf. *b* 23. Changeless and impassible, *De an.* i. 3. 407 *a* 33; *Phys.* vii. 3. 247 *b* 1; 247 *a* 28. Zeller, *Aristotle*, II, 94, n. 2.

[3] *De an.* iii. 4. 430 *a* 23.   [4] *De an.* ii. 2. 413 *b* 26.

[5] Stob. *Ecl.* i. 796. Cf. Ps. Plut. *Vit. Hom.* C 217, τὴν ψυχὴν οἱ Στωικοὶ ὁρίζονται πνεῦμα συμφυὲς καὶ ἀναθυμίασιν αἰσθητικὴν ἀναπτομένην ἀπὸ τῶν ἐν σώματι ὑγρῶν.

[6] For primitive views see Hicks, *Aristotle's De Anima*, p. xx. For the Stoic view see Galen, *Hippocr. et Plat.*, II, 8, p. 282; Zeller, *Stoics, Epicureans, and Skeptics*, p. 212, n. 2.

[7] Zeller, *op. cit.*, p. 215, n. 2.

[8] Plut. *Plac.* iv. 4. 2; Zeller, *op. cit.*, p. 214, n. 2 and p. 215, n. 2.

[9] See Alex. Aphr., *De an.* 146 where the Stoic opinion is controverted; cf. Tertullian, *De an.* 14; Zeller, *op. cit.*, p. 215, n. 2.

[10] Zeller, *op. cit.*, p. 214.   [11] Seneca *Epist.* 92. 1.

marked respectively by ἕξις, φύσις, ψυχή, and ψυχὴ λογική.[1] ἕξις is the characteristic of inorganic things. It is defined as a πνεῦμα συνεκτικόν.[2] Plants are distinguished by φύσις, the forming or reproductive power, defined in Diogenes Laertius, vii. 148. ἔστι δὲ φύσις ἕξις ἐξ αὑτῆς κινουμένη κατὰ σπερματικοὺς λόγους, ἀποτελοῦσά τε καὶ συνέχουσα τὰ ἐξ αὐτῆς ἐν ὡρισμένοις χρόνοις.[3] Animals have ψυχή, defined by Philo (*Leg. all.* 2:23) in a passage which is strongly influenced by Stoic phraseology, as φύσις προσειληφυῖα φαντασίαν καὶ ὁρμήν. The resemblances to Plato and Aristotle in this classification are obvious.

The teaching of Philo can now be seen in its historical connections. In the study of his teaching it is important to notice that he uses the word ψυχή in three different senses. It sometimes means that which distinguishes the principle of life in animals from plants and inorganic matter. The whole range of existence is divided in Stoic fashion in *Quod Deus sit* 35 ff. according to the presence of ἕξις, φύσις, ψυχή, and ψυχὴ λογική. ἕξις, the characteristic of inorganic things, is defined as a πνεῦμα ἀνάστρεφον ἐφ' ἑαυτό. "For it begins from the middle, extends to the extremities and, when it has touched the outermost boundaries, it turns back again until it comes to the place from which it set out." φύσις is the distinguishing feature of plants. It is said, following Aristotle, to be composed of θρεπτική, μεταβλητική, αὐξητική.[4] ψυχή is assigned to animals. It differs from φύσις in the possession of αἴσθησις, φαντασία, and ὁρμή, corresponding to the Aristotelian αἴσθησις, ὄρεξις and φαντασία. (*De an.* 434 a 1). αἴσθησις is a prerequisite of φαντασία.[5] The highest class is characterized by νοῦς.[6] In the fourfold division, ψυχή stands, then, for the special functions which distinguish animals from plants. It is in the sense of the animal soul that Philo says that ψυχή has its essence in blood. He adopts the Stoic teaching only in this sense and not for the ψυχὴ λογική.[7]

[1] Zeller, *op. cit.*, p. 208, n. 3.

[2] Ritter and Preller, 506 a; cf. in 505 a Plut. *Stoic. rep.* 43. 2, p. 1053 f. οὐδὲν ἄλλο τὰς ἕξεις πλὴν ἀέρας εἶναί φησιν (ὁ Χρύσιππος)· ὑπὸ τούτων γὰρ συνέχεται τὰ σώματα· καὶ τοῦ ποιὸν ἕκαστον εἶναι τῶν ἕξει συνεχομένων αἴτιος ὁ συνέχων ἀήρ ἐστιν . . . . 4. τὰς δὲ ποιότητας πνεύματα οὔσας καὶ τόνους ἀερώδεις οἷς ἂν ἐγγένωνται μέρεσι τῆς ὕλης εἰδοποιεῖν ἕκαστα καὶ σχηματίζειν.

[3] Ritter and Preller, *op. cit.*, 500 a.

[4] Cf. Aristotle *De an.* 413 a 24, κίνησις ἡ κατὰ τροφὴν καὶ φθίσις τε καὶ αὔξησις.

[5] *Quod Deus sit* 41 f. Cf. *De an.* 428 b 11, ἡ δὲ φαντασία κίνησίς τις δοκεῖ εἶναι καὶ οὐκ ἄνευ αἰσθήσεως γίγνεσθαι.

[6] Cf. *Quod det. pot.* 141; *De mund.* 5 (M. 606).

[7] *Sp. leg.* 4:122, 123; *Frg.* in M. 668; *Quis rer. div.* 54 ff., 64, 185; *Sp. leg.* 1:205; *Quod det. pot.* 84.

But the word is used by Philo in other senses. Two meanings are distinguished in *Quis rer. div.* 55. It may mean ἡ ὅλη ψυχή, the living principle generally, or it may stand for τὸ ἡγεμονικὸν αὐτῆς μέρος, ὃ κυρίως εἰπεῖν ψυχὴ ψυχῆς ἐστι.[1] So in the case of ὀφθαλμός, the same word may mean the whole eye or the chief part of the eye, that by which we see.[2] The essence of the whole is blood, that of the most hegemonic part is the πνεῦμα θεῖον.[3] The ὅλη ψυχή is the house of the intellect.[4] It is the principle of life, of thought, and of all human action.[5] It is the pilot of the body as the intellect is its pilot.[6]

The soul in the sense of ὅλη ψυχή is divided into parts called also functions, or powers.[7] According to one method of division, there are seven parts, reason, speech and the five senses; so in *De Ab.* 29 f. Eight are mentioned in *Quis rer. div.* 232 and *Mut. nom.* 110 f., the undivided reasoning part and the unreasoning, divided into the five senses, speech, and the reproductive faculty. The most common division is into the two parts, the reasoning and the unreasoning.[8] The Platonic division into reason, spirit, and passion is also adopted at times and, following Plato, the reason is located in the head, spirit in the breast, and passion about the navel and the diaphragm.[9] The Aristotelian division into the

[1] See also *Quis rer. div.* 181 (cf. Plato *Theaet.* 191 C); *Decal.* 134; *Sp. leg.* 2:202; *Quis rer. div.* 106–11.

[2] *De op. mund.* 66.

[3] Bréhier, *Allegories*, in his note to *Leg. all.* 3:161, says that we have in this passage a criticism of the Stoic belief that the soul was an emanation from blood, and accuses Philo of inconsistency. But ψυχή is here used in the sense of λογική ψυχή and, consistently with Philo's usual view, is described as a πνεῦμα θεῖον. Cf. for the division into ψυχὴ λογική and σῶμα *De op. mund.* 135; *Quis rer. div.* 155; *De cherub.* 32; *Quod det. pot.* 6; *De op. mund.* 46; Hatch, *Essays in Biblical Greek* (Oxford, 1889), p. 110.

[4] *Somn.* 2:173.   [5] *Decal.* 60.

[6] *De Ab.* 272.

[7] δύναμις in this sense goes back to Plato. Cf. *Rep.* 477 C; *Protag.* 330 A; *Char.* 168 D; *Theaet.* 185 C. Cf. in Philo αἴσθησις as a δύναμις—*Leg. all.* 2:37.

[8] *Quod det. pot.* 82, 92; *Conf. ling.* 54, 55, 111, 176; *De sac. A. et C.* 112; *Quis rer. div.* 132; *De sob.* 18; *Sp. leg.* 1:201, 333, 3:99; *De cong.* 26 f.; *Fug. et Inv.* 24; *Somn.* 2:151; *Leg. all.* 2:6. Cf. Plato *Rep.* 605 B.

[9] *Sp. leg.* 4:92, 93; *Mig. Ab.* 66–68; *Leg. all.* 1:70; 3:115; *Sp. leg.* 1:145–50. Cf. *Conf. ling.* 21; *De virt.* 13. Cf. Plato *Phaedr.* 246 A, 253 C; *Tim.* 69 E. Philo is uncertain whether to locate the mind in the brain or in the heart. See *Sp. leg.* 1:213; *De sac. A. et C.* 136; *Quod det. pot.* 90; *De post. C.* 137. For the Stoic location of τὸ ἡγεμονικόν in the breast cf. Zeller, *Stoics, Epicureans, and Skeptics*, p. 213, n. 2.

nutritive, sensitive, and reasoning souls also occurs.[1] At times again, the soul is regarded as a unity and the parts are functions.[2]

There is one remarkable passage, *Quis rer. div.* 225, in which Philo refers to ψυχή as having been shown previously to be divided into three parts and each of these into two. The reference seems to be to *Quis rer. div.* 106-11, where men are said to receive from God a deposit for which they must render an account. This deposit consists of ψυχή, αἴσθησις and λόγος. The context shows that ψυχή means here intelligence or reason, and λόγος means speech. Later in the same treatise (§ 132), he says that these three are each divided into two parts, ψυχή into the rational and irrational parts, αἴσθησις into φαντασία καταληπτική and ἀκατάληπτος, λόγος into true and false.

This summary is sufficient to show how unimportant for Philo all divisions are except the main one which gives the two parts, rational and irrational. The exigencies of the allegorical method lead him to adopt now one, now another point of view. It is not sufficient ground on which to base an accusation of looseness of thought or a careless eclecticism that in a matter such as this Philo knows the various speculations and can adopt them as his literary method demands.

The one distinction which persists throughout is the one which is important for ethics, the distinction, that is, between the rational and the irrational parts of the soul. In exalting the reason over the sensual, he draws on many sources for his language. Following Plato, he describes it as an impression of the archetypal seal[3] and as alone of the parts of our composite nature created by God,[4] immortal,[5]

[1] *De op. mund.* 67.

[2] See *Somn.* 2:145, 151, 215; *De Ab.* 29 f. (where νοῦς is a δύναμις of the soul). The Platonic divisions λόγος, θυμός, ἐπιθυμία, are described as δυνάμεις in *De virt.* 13. For δυνάμεις applied to the rational and irrational divisions of the soul see *Mig. Ab.* 119, 213; *Quis rer. div.* 73; *Somn.* 2:151; *Conf. ling.* 111. Philo also speaks of the senses as δυνάμεις of the mind; see *De Ab.* 73.

[3] νόμισμα, *Quod Deus sit* 105; *De plant.* 18. ἐκμαγεῖον, *De op. mund.* 146; *Quis rer. div.* 231. ὁ ἀνθρώπινος νοῦς πρὸς ἀρχέτυπον ἰδέαν, τὸν ἀνωτάτω λόγον, τυπωθείς—*Sp. leg.* 3:207; cf. *Sp. leg.* 1:81. τὸν αὐτοῦ λόγον .... ἀφ' οὗ καθάπερ ἀρχετύπου γέγονεν ὁ ἀνθρώπινος νοῦς—*De praem.* 163; cf. *Sp. leg.* 1:171 (ἐμορφώθη). ἀπεικόνισμα καὶ μίμημα τῆς ἀϊδίου καὶ εὐδαίμονος ἰδέας—*Decal.* 134. Cf. θεοείκελον, Plato *Rep.* 501 B. For an account of the figures by which Plato seeks to represent the relation between the idea and the copy see Adam, *Republic of Plato*, II, 172. For the notion that the particular is a copy cf. *Rep.* 592 B, 596 B, 597 B.

[4] The lower part of the soul is created by the instrumentality of inferior powers—*Leg. all.* 1:41; *Fug. et Inv.* 69; *Conf. ling.* 179. Cf. *Tim.* 41 C-42 E and 69 C.

[5] ἀθάνατον, *Tim.* 69 C. Cf. *Mig. Ab.* 185. See for similar idea *Fug. et Inv.* 69.

divine[1] and heavenly. Aristotle is drawn upon for the expression that the reason may be a πέμπτη οὐσία superior to the four elements.[2] The Stoics furnish the metaphors by which it is described as a ray[3] or emanation[4] of the divine. The Book of Genesis furnishes the description of this part of the soul as a breath of God.[5] The Platonic exaltation of reason over passion is the prominent notion in all these figures.

Philo is, as we have shown, in accord with Plato in making the chief division of the soul that into reason and the irrational parts, and exalting the reason into a different category. In this he is also in harmony with the Stoics. In the two points in which the Stoics differ from Plato, he is in accord with the latter. These two points are dogmatism and materialism.

Philo indicates clearly his lack of dogmatism. The mind or soul or reason in us is, he says, a mystery. "The mind in each of us can comprehend all other things but is unable to know itself. For let it say what it is and whence, whether it is spirit or blood or fire or some other substance, or only so. much, whether it is corporeal or incorporeal" (*Leg. all.* 1:91).[6] So, in *Somn.* 1:30–33, νοῦς is said to be unknown in its essence. We are ignorant, too, of when it enters the body and where it lives in the body. See also *Mut. nom.* 10.

This attitude of conscious recognition of the limits of human thought is genuinely Platonic,[7] especially as it goes with a conviction that the

[1] θεῖον, *Tim.* 69 D; *Rep.* 589 D E; cf. *Rep.* 501 B. See Philo *Leg. all.* 2:95, δύο γένη φορεῖ ἡ ψυχή, τὸ μὲν θεῖον, τὸ δὲ φθαρτόν. Cf. *Quis rer. div.* 55; *De gig.* 60; also θεοειδές in *Quis rer. div.* 65 and Plato *Rep.* 501 B. οὐράνιος, *Quis rer. div.* 64.

[2] *Quis rer. div.* 283. Cf. Zeller, *Phil. der Griech.*, Vol. II, Part II, pp. 483 ff. This passage is discussed below on pp. 56 ff.

[3] ἀπαύγασμα, *De op. mund.* 146; *Somn.* 1:112. Cf. the Stoic use of the word ἀπόρροια; see Zeller, *Phil. der Griech.*, Vol. III, Part I, p. 200, n. 2; Empedocles, in Diels, *Frg. d. Vorsok.*, I, 162, l. 32. See also Diels, *Dox. Gr.*, 505, 6. For Philo see p. 56 below.

[4] ἀπόσπασμα, *Quis rer. div.* 283; *De op. mund.* 146; *Somn.* 1:34; *Quod det. pot.* 90. In the last passage Philo guards against the inference which might be drawn from the term, that the essence of man is separate from that of God—τέμνεται γὰρ οὐδὲν τοῦ θείου κατ' ἀπάρτησιν ἀλλὰ μόνον ἐκτείνεται. For the Stoic use of the word see Diog. Laert. vii. 143 and M. Antonin. v, 27; Zeller, *Phil. der Griech.*, Vol. III, Part I, p. 200, n. 2.

[5] The lower part arises from the blood. Compare the Stoic doctrine given above, p. 49, n. 5. See *Quis rer. div.* 55 f., 64, 185; *Somn.* 1:146, 181; *De op. mund.* 135; *De Ab.* 258; *Sp. leg.* 4:123; *Frg.* in M. 668.

[6] Compare the phraseology of *Phaedo* 96 B, πότερον τὸ αἷμά ἐστιν ᾧ φρονοῦμεν ἢ ὁ ἀὴρ ἢ τὸ πῦρ; ἢ τούτων μὲν οὐδέν.

[7] See Shorey, *Unity of Plato's Thought*, p. 45 and n. 313.

reality of our life is not found in the material, in the life of sense, but in what we call the life of the spirit. This point of view might also be described as Aristotelian, for Aristotle is essentially in accord with Plato here. In the *De anima*, he holds firmly to the notion of a separable, pure activity of thought, but he insists that it has no bodily organ and he leaves unanswered the question of its relation to the world of sense.[1]

As regards materialism, Philo was convinced that the soul is akin to God, a part of him. The epithets θεῖον and ἄφθαρτον indicate this.[2] The word ἀπόσπασμα emphasizes the same idea. Philo carefully guards the last expression to show that he does not mean to imply any separation from God.[3] In a number of passages, however, the language seems to imply that Philo has, for the moment at least, abandoned Platonism and adopted the materialistic conception of the Stoics. One group of these passages consists of those in which he uses the expression πνεῦμα or πνεῦμα θεῖον of the soul.[4] Now among the Stoics such a term implies materialism, and the inference seems at first sight irresistible that Philo too is using it in a materialistic sense. So Hatch (*Essays in Biblical Greek*, p. 126), says "the conception of πνεῦμα may be regarded as being closely analogous to the modern conception of 'force,' and especially to that form of the conception which makes no distinction of essence between 'mind-force' and other kinds of force, such as light or electricity. It is analogous but not identical: for force is conceived to be immaterial, whereas πνεῦμα, however subtle, is still material."

There is no doubt that Philo does use the word in the sense of the Stoic materialists. The passages are quoted by Hatch (*loc. cit.*). ἕξις, the quality of cohesion in bodies, is, for example, a πνεῦμα ἀνάστρεφον ἐφ' ἑαυτό (*Quod Deus sit* 35). In *De op. mund.* 67, φύσις is said to mould τὴν δὲ πνευματικὴν εἰς τὰς τῆς ψυχῆς δυνάμεις, τήν τε θρεπτικὴν καὶ τὴν αἰσθητικήν. Here the "pneumatic essence" is clearly air, contrasted with τὴν ὑγρὰν οὐσίαν, out of which the body is made. The materialistic conception is probably, though not so certainly, present in the account of the psychology of sensation where Philo makes large use of Stoic language. The mind, he says (*Fug. et Inv.* 182), extends a seeing πνεῦμα to the eyes, a hearing πνεῦμα to the ears, and so with the other senses.

---

[1] See Shorey, Hastings' *Encyc. of Relig. and Eth.*, IX, 862 b; Hicks, *De Anima of Aristotle*, pp. lviii–lxix.

[2] See above, p. 52, n. 5, and p. 53, n. 1. [3] See above, p. 53, n. 4.

[4] For Philo's use of πνεῦμα see Burton, *Spirit, Soul, and Flesh* (Chicago, 1918), pp. 157–60; Hatch, *Essays in Biblical Greek*, pp. 124 ff.

MAN'S SOUL AND ITS POWERS 55

The πνεῦμα thus extended from the mind is analogous to the πνεῦμα of God which constitutes the essence of the mind itself (*Leg. all.* 1:40). God breathes only into the hegemonic part of the soul. Into the other parts He does not deign to breathe. Those lower parts are breathed into by the νοῦς just as the νοῦς itself is breathed into by God. It is probable that the πνεύματα which constitute the organs of sense are to be regarded here as material. It is to be noted that the relation of God to the νοῦς is said to be analogous to the relation of νοῦς and the various senses, not identical with it.

In any discussion of materialism in connection with doctrines of the soul, it must be kept in mind that the relationship between God and the individual soul and between the soul and the body is one which can only be represented by metaphors drawn from the material world. There is always the possibility that the language may be merely metaphorical. In the case of Philo, his insistence on the transcendence of God over matter and on the kinship of the soul to Him makes it necessary that we accept the materialistic interpretation of such passages only if we are compelled to do so. Now in *De gig.* 22 f., Philo makes it clear that πνεῦμα does not necessarily have any materialistic suggestions. The words πνεῦμα θεοῦ, he tells us, are used in two senses. In one sense the expression means the air that flows from the earth. It is in this sense that it is used in Gen. 1:2 where the πνεῦμα θεοῦ is said to be borne over the face of the waters. In its second use, it is equivalent to ἡ ἀκήρατος ἐπιστήμη ἧς πᾶς ὁ σοφὸς εἰκότως μετέχει. The Scripture, Philo says, makes this clear in the verse ἀνεκάλεσεν ὁ θεὸς τὸν Βεσελεὴλ καὶ ἐνέπλησεν αὐτὸν πνεύματος θείου, σοφίας, συνέσεως, ἐπιστήμης, ἐπὶ πάντι ἔργῳ διανοεῖσθαι. These passages show beyond a doubt that the word admits of an interpretation that is opposed to the Stoic materialism.

It seems to settle the question in favor of Philo's adoption of materialistic notions that in *Fug. et Inv.* 134 the νοῦς is called ἔνθερμον καὶ πεπυρωμένον πνεῦμα. A close examination of the context shows, however, that it admits a metaphorical interpretation. The phrase occurs in an explanation of the question asked by Isaac when Abraham was about to offer him as a sacrifice. "Behold the fire and the wood, but where is the sheep for the offering?" (Gen. 22:7 f.). The fire, Philo tells us, means δρῶν αἴτιον, the wood τὸ πάσχον or ὕλη, the sheep τὸ ἀποτέλεσμα. These terms are Stoic, but the explanation which follows comes from Plato's *Theaetetus*, through Aristotle. In his half-serious exposition of the Protagorean theory of sensation in *Theaetetus* 153 D f., Plato says that when sight, flowing from the eye, meets something commensurate with it, the eye becomes a seeing eye and the object perceptible. In the *De anima* 417 a 6 f., Aristotle develops the idea of the eye which becomes the seeing eye. He says that the faculty of sensation (τὸ αἰσθητικόν) exists not in actuality but only in potentiality: διὸ καθάπερ τὸ καυστὸν οὐ καίεται αὐτὸ καθ' αὑτὸ ἄνευ τοῦ καυστικοῦ· ἔκαιε γὰρ ἂν ἑαυτό, καὶ οὐθὲν ἐδεῖτο τοῦ ἐντελεχείᾳ πυρὸς ὄντος. It is this passage that Philo has in mind in developing the allegory here. The series in Aristotle is τὸ καυστόν, τὸ καυστικόν, τὸ καίεσθαι, representing τὸ αἰσθητόν, τὸ αἰσθητικόν, τὸ αἰσθάνεσθαι. Philo says that the fire might be νοῦς ἔνθερμον καὶ πεπυρωμένον πνεῦμα, in which case the wood means τὰ νοητά and the sheep τὸ νοεῖν. The context here would not warrant our pressing Philo's language. In view of the general opposition to materialism in his writings, and in view of the metaphorical character of the passage, it is much more probable that the Stoic expression is a mere rhetorical flourish used in the interests of the allegorical interpretation. This figurative interpretation of the passage is supported by *De gig.* 25, in the context of the passage discussed on p. 55 above. Discussing the verse "I will take of the spirit that is upon thee and put it upon the seventy elders," (Num. 11:17), Philo says that we must not suppose that there is any cutting off or dispersion in this case, "but such a separation as would take place from a fire,[1] which, even if it kindles countless torches, remains not a whit lessened and just as it was before." It would be quite in Philo's manner to use a metaphor here instead of a simile and speak of the πνεῦμα as a fire.

Another passage which is taken to imply materialism[2] is *Quis rer. div.* 283. It occurs in an interpretation of "Thou shalt come to thy fathers," in Gen. 15:15. Philo says that some have interpreted the word fathers to mean elements. So we shall render up to the various elements the materials of which our bodies are composed. τὸ δὲ νοερὸν καὶ οὐράνιον τῆς ψυχῆς γένος πρὸς αἰθέρα· τὸν καθαρώτατον ὡς πατέρα ἀφίξεται. πέμπτη γάρ, ὡς ὁ τῶν ἀρχαίων λόγος, ἔστω τις οὐσία κυκλοφορητική, τῶν τεττάρων κατὰ τὸ κρεῖττον διαφέρουσα, ἐξ ἧς οἵ τε ἀστέρες καὶ ὁ σύμπας οὐρανὸς ἔδοξε γεγενῆσθαι ἧς κατ' ἀκόλουθον θετέον καὶ τὴν ἀνθρωπίνην ψυχὴν ἀπόσπασμα. The reference in τῶν ἀρχαίων is to Aristotle. See Zeller, *Phil. der Griech.*, Vol. II, Part II, pp. 483 ff. The passage is not a dogmatic statement of Philo's fixed belief; note ἔστω. It is consciously mythological. Philo is fond of talking in this mythological fashion of the heaven as the

[1] Cf. ἀπαύγασμα above, p. 53.
[2] Hatch, *loc. cit.*

abode of pure spirits,[1] as the purest of all substances,[2] and contrasting its stability, permanence and order with the confusion of earthly things.[3] It is an unknown element[4] and it is impossible to say whether it is crystal, purest fire, or πέμπτον κυκλοφορικὸν σῶμα μηδενὸς τῶν τεττάρων στοιχείων μετέχον. The feeling about the heaven which gives rise to the praises it receives is due, as in Plato, to the exhibition of ordered movement there made visible.

The sight conducted upwards by light and beholding the nature of the stars and their harmonious movement, the well-ordered revolutions of the fixed stars and the planets, some moving in the sphere of the same and others in the sphere of the different, using twofold movements; and beholding too the dances of them all harmonised by the laws of perfect music, afforded an ineffable delight and pleasure to the soul. And the soul, receiving these spectacles in continuous succession, began to have an insatiate desire for beholding. And then, as is customary, it began to try to find the essence of these visible things and whether they are unbegotten or whether they received a beginning of birth and what is the fashion of their motion and what are the causes by which each is governed. And from the inquiry into these things there came philosophy, than which no more perfect good has come into the life of man.[5]

This is a common topic in Philo.[6] The whole notion of the purity of heaven is based on Plato's *Timaeus* 47 A and, as Philo's agnostic utterances show, is a mythical statement used in the context to justify for the emotions the cardinal point in Philo's faith that the human soul has its footing somewhere beyond time and that man can defy the allurements of appetite and ambition and find his true satisfaction in the life of the spirit. The predominant ethical interest again recalls Plato.

The Stoic word τόνος with its derivatives is frequent in Philo's descriptions of the soul and its relation to the body.[7] These expressions have a literal, material significance in the Stoics but they occur as metaphors in Plato[8] and Aristotle[9] and they cannot be pressed in Philo and made to serve as proofs of his adoption of the Stoic theory.

[1] *De op. mund.* 27, 36, 37; *Sp. leg.* 1:88; *De virt.* 73, 85; *De praem* 1; *Decal.* 134, 155; *Cong.* 50; *V.M.* 2:194.
[2] *De op. mund.* 27, 55; *Sp. leg.* 1:66; *Somn.* 1:34–36; *V.M.* 2:194; *Sp. leg.* 4:235.
[3] *V.M.* 1:217; *De Ab.* 272; *Jos.* 145 ff.
[4] *Somn.* 1:21–24. [5] *De op. mund.* 54; cf. *Tim.* 47 A B.
[6] Cf. *De Ab.* 164; *Sp. leg.* 1:322, 339; 3:185 f., 192; *Frg.* in M. 665.
[7] Cf. for εὐτονία of the soul *De post. C.* 46; τῶν τόνων τῶν ψυχικῶν, 1 *Somn.* 88; νοεροὶ τόνοι, *De praem.* 21. See also *De praem.* 48; *Quaes. in Gen.* 1:10; *Leg. all.* 3:69; *Mig. Ab.* 9; *Jos.* 61.
[8] Cf. *Phaedo* 86 B; *Rep.* 581 B; *Theaet.* 186 C; *Tim.* 34 B; *Symp.* 186 B, 188 B.
[9] *Eth. Nic.* 1138 b 23.

In a previous part of this essay it has been shown that Philo is in close dependence on Plato in his doctrine of the descent of the soul.[1] The νοῦς or ψυχή which is incarnated in this or that man is seen upon earth in only part of its history. It is a part of the great company of angels who live in the air. Its descent to earth is due to the fact that it was somehow evil.[2] There are, however, varying degrees of wickedness. Some of the souls are swept away and overwhelmed by sense,[3] others rise into the region from whence they set out.[4]

The notion has been attributed to Philo that the human intelligence is itself earthly and corruptible and that immortality is acquired only by its transformation into pure intelligence.[5] The passage in *V.M.* 1:27 in which this teaching is said to be found shows in what sense Philo accepts this doctrine. He is there telling of the temperance and self-control Moses showed in his youth, which was so great that people wondered whether the mind that lived in his body was divine or human or mingled of the two. The passage means that men wondered whether Moses were not divinely inspired and his own intelligence displaced by the divine,[6] or else filled with a divine madness so that he had become more than man, though still less than God.[7] There is no support for Bréhier's theory that Philo thinks of the human mind that is exalted above sense as metamorphosed into a creative word.[8] The statement in *Leg. all.* 3:125 where the purified intelligence is said to wear the divine word means in the context that the completely pure man speaks for God. Philo is here explaining how Aaron is made priest and wears the λόγιον with its clearness and truth when he enters in before the Lord. The notion of metamorphosis is the common Greek mystic conception of ὁμοίωσις or even actual identity with the god attained in moments of inspiration. In Philo, as in Plato, this notion is moralized and means that the mind has risen above the distractions and temptations of sense.[9]

[1] See above, pp. 41-43.
[2] *De gig.* 16 f. These are the wicked δαίμονες.
[3] *De gig.* 15.
[4] *De gig.* 13 f.; *Cong.* 107 f.; *De praem.* 62.
[5] Bréhier, *Id. phil. et relig.*, p. 240. Cf. γεώδης νοῦς in *Leg. all.* 1:32-42.
[6] *Mig. Ab.* 114; *Sp. leg.* 4:49; *Quis rer. div.* 263-66.
[7] *Somn.* 2:188 f., 231 f.   [8] *Id. phil. et relig.*, pp. 240 f.
[9] See above, p. 23; Rohde, *Psyche*, II, 14 ff. Bréhier, *op. cit.*, pp. 240 and 246, thinks that the two notions of metamorphosis and moral purification are found nowhere outside of Philo except in the Egyptian Book of the Dead. But see Plato *Phaedr.* 249 C, 256 B; *Phaedo* 67 C; *Crat.* 403 E f.

MAN'S SOUL AND ITS POWERS

In the composite earthly being, the soul is lord and king[1] and plays there the part that God plays in the universe.[2] It inspires the irrational parts of the soul just as it is itself inspired by God.[3] It is the ever-moving source of motion.[4] It is surrounded by powers or senses as by a bodyguard.[5] It is a unity and yet extends to all the parts of the body.[6] It is an imitation of the Logos[7] and as such is called the man in our soul[8] in contrast to the beast which symbolizes the passions.[9]

Set over against the intelligence, though still regarded as a function of it, is αἴσθησις. This has two main aspects, called by Philo φαντασία and ὁρμή. The division originates with Aristotle's analysis in *De anima* iii. Suggestions of Aristotle's teaching are, however, to be found in Plato and it will make the meaning of the terms clearer if Plato's teaching is first described. αἴσθησις, or sensation, is said in *Sophist* 264 A "to originate a certain judgment of affirmation or denial which should be called φαντασία." The latter word is to be interpreted, we are told in the context, in connection with the word φαίνεται and is a mixture of αἴσθησις and δόξα. Plato's meaning is that φαντασία is an opinion in the mind resting on the uncriticised data of sense.[10] So in *Theaet.* 152 C we are told that in the case of hot, cold, and the like, φαντασία is the same as αἴσθησις. In *Theaet.* 161 E, φαντασίαι are coupled with δόξαι. Memory images and images of the "imagination," both go back ultimately to αἴσθησις,[11] so that in all cases φαντασία originates in αἴσθησις. It is

---

[1] *Sp. leg.* 1:258, 269; *De sac. A. et C.* 112; *De virt.* 30; *Frg.* M. 637; *Fug. et Inv.* 69; *V.M.* 2:211. Cf. Plato *Rep.* 605 B; *Phaedo* 80 A; *Phaedr.* 247 C.

[2] Like the sun, *De post. C.* 58; *Quis rer. div.* 89, 263. As Father, *Leg. all.* 3:225; *Mig. Ab.* 3. *De Ab.* 272; *De op. mund.* 69; Plato *Laws* 897 B.

[3] *Leg. all.* 1:40.

[4] *Incorr. mund.* 16 (M. 504); *De sac A. et C.* 127. Cf. *Phaedr.* 245 D E; *Laws* 896 E ff.

[5] *Quod det. pot.* 33, 85; *De op. mund.* 139; *Somn.* 1:27, 32; *Sp. leg.* 3:111, 4:92, 123.

[6] *De ag.* 30. The language here is Stoic.

[7] *Quis rer. div.* 231; cf. *ibid.* 56; *Sp. leg.* 1:81. See above, p. 38 with note 4.

[8] *Quod det. pot.* 22 f.; *De ag.* 9 ff.; *De plant.* 42; *Cong.* 97; *Fug. et Inv.* 71 f.; *Somn.* 1:215, 2:267.

[9] *De plant.* 43; *De eb.* 28; *Conf. ling.* 24; *Mig. Ab.* 152; cf. Plato *Rep.* 588 B-590 A, especially 589 D.

[10] Cf. *Theaet.* 179 C, τὸ παρὸν ἑκάστῳ πάθος ἐξ ὧν αἱ αἰσθήσεις καὶ αἱ κατὰ ταύτας δόξαι. *Charm.* 159 A, αἴσθησίν τινα παρέχειν ἐξ ἧς δόξα ἄν τίς σοι περὶ αὐτῆς εἴη.

[11] For memory images see *Phil.* 39 C; *Phaedo* 73 D; *Theaet.* 191 D; for images of the imagination, *Phil.* 39 C.

scarcely necessary to say that αἴσθησις in Plato includes pleasure and pain, as well as the presentation of the data on which judgments are based.[1]

Aristotle discusses φαντασία at length in *De anima* iii. 3. 427 b 27–429 a 9. It is the faculty in virtue of which we say that an image presents itself to us, a faculty or habit in virtue of which we judge and judge truly or falsely. He attacks the Platonic identification of φαντασία with αἴσθησις (*Theaet.* 152 C) on the ground that an image may present itself when sense is not active, as, for example, in dreams. Moreover the identification of φαντασία with αἴσθησις would involve the possibility that all animals (θηρία) possess φαντασία. The ant, the bee, and the grub do not possess it. Again, sensations, he tells us, are always true; φαντασίαι are for the most part false. In this sentence, which contradicts what he said above that φαντασία is the faculty or habit in virtue of which κρίνομεν καὶ ἀληθεύομεν καὶ ψευδόμεθα, Aristotle is obviously referring to the "painter" and the pictures he paints in *Philebus* 39 B–40 A. There the pictures (φαντάσματα) are contrasted with reality. However, Aristotle has made his point that φαντασία cannot be identified with αἴσθησις. He does not differ here from Plato. Professor Shorey points out (*Unity*, p. 49), that the *Theaetetus* "does not identify the words by using them once or twice as synonyms."

Aristotle next (428 a 16) shows that φαντασία cannot be identified with knowledge or intellect. These are always true, while φαντασία may be false. Is it, then, the same as δόξα?[2] Aristotle says that it is not. In the first place, opinion is attended by conviction (πίστις). No θηρίον ever has conviction, though many have φαντασία. πίστις implies persuasion (τὸ πεπεῖσθαι), persuasion implies λόγος. φαντασία is not, then, δόξα μετ' αἰσθήσεως nor δόξα δι' αἰσθήσεως.[3] Nor is it a συμπλοκὴ δόξης καὶ αἰσθήσεως.[4] For, if it is such a complex, it must be in cases where opinion and sense are directed to the same object. But "there are false imaginings of things concerning which we hold at the same time a true opinion."

Finished with his polemic, Aristotle proceeds to give his own conclusions (428 b 10). φαντασία, he says, seems to be a species of motion

[1] *Theaet.* 156 B; *Phil.* 34 A–C; Shorey, *Unity*, p. 47 and n. 336.

[2] Plato *Theaet.* 161 E.

[3] Cf. *Theaet.* 158 A, ὡς παντὸς μᾶλλον ἡμῖν ψευδεῖς αἰσθήσεις ἐν αὑτοῖς γιγνομένας καὶ πολλοῦ δεῖ τὰ φαινόμενα ἑκάστῳ ταῦτα καὶ εἶναι, and *Soph.* 264 A where φαντασία is a judgment present to the mind δι' αἰσθήσεως, while δόξα is a judgment ἐν ψυχῇ κατὰ διάνοιαν.

[4] Cf. σύμμιξις αἰσθήσεως καὶ δόξης, *Soph.* 264 A.

which does not arise apart from sensation. It can exist only in sentient beings and has the objects of sense for its objects. This motion may be produced by actual sensation. It admits of error even in cases such as this, for sensation is not always inerrant. Sensation of the objects of the special senses is always true or subject to the minimum of error. As to the whiteness of an object, for example, sense is never mistaken, but it may be mistaken as to whether the white object is a man or something else. It is also liable to error as to motion and magnitude. The φαντασίαι arising from these various types of sensation share the truth or falsehood of their cause. φαντασία is, then, a κίνησις generated by αἴσθησις when it is active. These imaginations remain in us and resemble the corresponding sensations.

But αἴσθησις has another aspect. "Sensation," Aristotle tells us (*De anima* 431 a 8 ff.), "is analogous to simple assertion or simple apprehension by thought." By "simple" he means "without predication." All that sensation can give us, for example, is the sensation of whiteness. It cannot tell us whether the white object is a man.[1] "But," he continues, "when the sensible thing is pleasant or painful, sensation by a kind of affirmation or denial seeks or avoids the object. To experience pleasure or pain is to function with the perceiving mean upon the good or evil as such."[2] "The perceiving mean" (τῇ αἰσθητικῇ μεσότητι) is Aristotle's phrase for the synthetic unity of sensation, the μίαν ἰδέαν εἴτε ψυχὴν εἴτε ὅ τι δεῖ καλεῖν in which all the senses are united, of which Plato speaks in *Theaet.* 184 D.[3] "It is in this," he continues, that is to say, in the functioning of the perceiving mean upon the good or evil as such, "that actual avoidance and actual appetition (ὄρεξις) consist: nor is the appetitive faculty distinct from the faculty of avoidance, nor either from the sensitive faculty; though logically they are different."[4] There are, then, two activities of sensation, φαντασία and the activity which seeks or avoids. Sensation does more than present an image to the mind; in relation to the good and evil it also judges.

[1] *De an.* 430 b 25–30.

[2] *De an.* 431 a 10, καὶ ἔστι τὸ ἥδεσθαι καὶ λυπεῖσθαι τὸ ἐνεργεῖν τῇ αἰσθητικῇ μεσότητι πρὸς τὸ ἀγαθὸν ἢ κακόν, ᾗ τοιαῦτα. Cf. *Rep.* 583 E, καὶ μὴν τό γε ἡδὺ ἐν ψυχῇ γιγνόμενον καὶ τὸ λυπηρὸν κίνησίς τις ἀμφοτέρω ἔστον. Hicks, *Aristotle's De Anima*, p. xxxvi, points out that "energy" is Aristotle's word for the Platonic "motion."

[3] It is discussed and defined by Aristotle in *De an.* 426 b 8–427 a 15. In potentiality, it is each of two opposites since it can be moved by both sweet and bitter, and it is in this sense that it is called a mean.

[4] Translation by Hicks, *Aristotle's De Anima*, p. 141, adapted.

The doctrine of the Stoics is in accord with that of Plato and Aristotle to this extent, that αἴσθησις originates φαντασία, and through φαντασία gives rise also to desire and its opposite. φαντασία is identified with the εἴδωλον of *Theaet.* 191 D. Zeno declared that φαντασία was a τύπωσις ἐν ψυχῇ,[1] and this definition is adopted by his followers in the Stoic school. Sextus Empiricus says that Cleanthes understood τὴν τύπωσιν κατὰ εἰσοχήν τε καὶ ἐξοχήν, ὥσπερ καὶ διὰ τῶν δακτυλίων γινομένην τοῦ κηροῦ τύπωσιν.[2] The language here is parallel with that of Plato, *Theaet.* 191 D, ἀποτυποῦσθαι ὥσπερ δακτυλίων σημεῖα ἐνσημαινομένους, but the criticism by Chrysippus, quoted in the context in Empiricus, shows that it was taken in a materialistic sense. According to this view, Chrysippus said, it would be necessary for the soul to receive at once many different forms if it had to retain the different notions at the same time. He interpreted τύπωσις as ἑτεροίωσις. This is described as a πάθος ἐν τῇ ψυχῇ γιγνόμενον.[3] These πάθη come διὰ the various senses.[4]

ὁρμή is the Stoic rendering of the Aristotelian words ὄρεξις or τὸ ὀρεκτικόν. As in Aristotle, this is roused by φαντασία.[5] If the desire is excessive, it is called a passion (πάθος). Such a desire does not submit to reason and is contrary to nature.[6] The πρώτη ὁρμή is the impulse the creature has toward self-preservation and self-gratification.[7]

Philo's account of φαντασία and ὁρμή, the πρώτη ὁρμή, the relation between ὁρμή and πάθος, is Stoic throughout. In the account of φαντασία he uses the Platonic figure of the wax tablet which plays so large a part in the Stoic theories, but in Philo there is a significant omission of the phrases by which the Stoics sought to enforce the materialistic interpretation. He does not mention τύπωσις κατὰ εἰσοχήν τε καὶ ἐξοχήν,[8] nor does he discuss the question whether or not τύπωσις may not be ἑτεροίωσις. The most detailed statement is to be found in *Quod Deus sit* 43 f. φαντασία, Philo says in this passage, is a τύπωσις ἐν ψυχῇ.

For each of the senses like a ring or seal stamps the peculiar impress of the things it brings in. The νοῦς, like wax, receives the impression and guards it well until forgetfulness, memory's opponent, smooths the mark and makes it dull or quite obliterates it. The representation affects the soul either in accordance with the soul's nature or else in a manner different from

---

[1] Arnim, *Stoic. Vet Frag.*, I, 58.
[2] Arnim, *op. cit.*, II, 56.   [3] Arnim, *op. cit.*, II, 54.
[4] *Ibid.* For a discussion of the Stoic doctrine see Zeller, *Stoics, Epicureans, and Skeptics*, pp. 78 f. with notes.
[5] Arnim, *op. cit.*, III, 169.   [7] *Ibid.*, III, 178; Zeller, *op. cit.*, p. 226 with n. 2.
[6] *Ibid.*, I, 205, 206.   [8] Cf. Arnim, *op. cit.*, II, 56.

MAN'S SOUL AND ITS POWERS 63

it.[1] This experience is called ὁρμή, which is defined as a πρώτη κίνησις of the soul. It is by the possession of these, (φαντασία and ὁρμή), that animals are superior to plants.

The language of *Theaet.* 191 D is echoed in many other passages.[2] The relation between αἴσθησις and φαντασία is indicated in *Leg. all.* 3:108, τὰ σώματα φαντασιούμεθα δι' αἰσθήσεως. αἴσθησις is used loosely as equivalent to φαντασία in *Quis rer. div.* 132, where it is divided in Stoic fashion into φαντασία καταληπτική and φαντασία ἀκατάληπτος.[3] While Philo in all this part of his teaching uses Stoic vocabulary, he does not depart from consistent Platonism. Stoicism is a development from Platonism and, in the one point in which the Stoics differ from Plato, in their materialism, his language admits of a figurative interpretation as fully as does that of Plato.

Philo's account of the physiology of sensation corresponds to that of the Stoics. They taught that from the ἡγεμονικόν to the various organs of sense πνεύματα are extended. The πνεῦμα of sight is met in the eye by an effluence from the object. Sight takes places when the ἡγεμονικόν imparts a movement of tension to the seeing πνεῦμα.[4] Philo's account is similar. There are three terms, he says, that are connected like a chain— the mind, the sense, the object. The sense does not act of itself. It must be roused to activity by the mind. Mind extends itself to sense and then rouses sense to grasp the object. The mind cannot function in perception unless God "moistens and rains upon the sensible object." The mind is the active principle in the subject; the senses are passive and quiet until moved by the mind.[5]

In *Theaet.* 156 DE Plato gives an ironical, half-serious exposition of the theory of Protagoras, which it is worth while to compare with the statements of Philo. Sensation, Plato says, arises when sight, flowing from the eye, meets with something commensurate with it. The eye then becomes a seeing eye and the object becomes perceptible. So in the *Timaeus* 45 C D he says that sight is due to a ῥεῦμα ὄψεως issuing

---

[1] Platonic. Cf. *Tim.* 64 C D; Brett, *History of Psychology*, p. 87.

[2] See *De mund.* (M. 606); *De ag.* 16; *Mut. nom.* 212; *Quis rer. div.* 181, 294; *Leg. all.* 1:30.

[3] Diog. Laert. vii. 46. See above, p. 52.

[4] Arnim, *op. cit.*, II, 864, 866, 867.

[5] Cf. *Leg. all.* 1:28–30; 2:35–45, where αἴσθησις καθ' ἕξιν, a δύναμις of νοῦς, is made into αἴσθησις καθ' ἐνέργειαν by being roused to motion and is extended μέχρι τῆς σαρκὸς καὶ τῶν αἰσθητικῶν ἀγγείων. Cf. *Leg. all.* 3:49 f. where αἴσθησις is a δύναμις of νοῦς.

from the eyes and striking some external substance. This contact sets up vibrations which are carried back to the mind.[1] Philo's view differs in that he regards the ῥεῦμα ὄψεως as extending from the mind, where it is αἴσθησις καθ' ἕξιν, to the eye where it becomes αἴσθησις καθ' ἐνέργειαν by the activity of the mind itself. The ῥεῦμα ὄψεως is, in fact, νοῦς or a "ductile power" of it,[2] not light, as it is in the *Timaeus*. Here Philo is in accord with the Stoics, not with Plato.[3] Yet elsewhere he gives an account which exactly corresponds with that of Plato. There is stored up in the eye light that is akin to the light of the sun and sight originates by the σύνοδος καὶ δεξίωσις of the light from the sun and that from the eye.[4] Objects, the eye, and light are needed for vision.[5]

Another account still is given in *Leg. all.* 3:56 ff. Here sense-perception is said to act independently of the mind and even against its bidding. The eye cannot but see if the sight comes in contact with the external object. The mind and the sense then act concurrently. This is Plato's teaching in *Timaeus* 42 A and 43 B C.[6] The mind is in a certain sense at the mercy of external things, for if sense receives an impression, the mind too receives it. For ordinary purposes, sense gives a true impression of the object.[7]

On the whole, Philo's account is Platonic. For both authors, the mind in the body is forced into union with sensation[8] and is dependent on the senses for its knowledge of the external world.[9] For both, again, sense in itself does nothing. Philo repeats the statement of the *Theaetetus* that the mind sees through the eye; the eye alone cannot see.[10] Where

---

[1] Cf. *Phil.* 34 A.   [2] *Leg. all.* 1:30.

[3] See Diog. Laert. vii. 52 (Arnim, *op. cit.*, II, 71), a passage referred to by Bréhier, *Allegories*, n. on *Leg. all.* 1:28-30.

[4] *Quod Deus sit* 79. Cf. *Tim.* 45 C.

[5] *De sac. A. et C.* 36; *De eb.* 190 f.; *De aet. m.* 86; *Sp. leg.* 4:60; *Mig. Ab.* 40. Cf. Plato *Rep.* 507 D E; *Tim.* 67 C ff.

[6] See also *Phil.* 34 A.

[7] A similar account is given in *Quaes. in Gen.* 1:37; *Sp. leg.* 3:177.

[8] *Somn.* 1:246; 2:230, 256; *De Ab.* 236-40, 243 f.; *Leg. all.* 3:220 f.; *Mig. Ab.* 204; *De eb.* 70, 101; *Cong.* 59, 81; *De praem.* 121; *Fug. et Inv.* 91, 158; *Quis rer. div.* 272 f. Cf. Plato *Phaedo* 65 B-67 B; *Phaedr.* 256 B.

[9] *Quis rer. div.* 53, 110, 315; *Cong.* 20 f.; *Frg.* in M. 665; *Somn.* 1:27; *Leg. all.* 2:7; *De op. mund.* 166; *De cherub.* 58; *Mut. nom.* 111; *Quod Deus sit* 41 f.; *Fug. et Inv.* 134; *Mig. Ab.* 103. See Plato *Theaet.* 184 C D, 185 A, 201 B; *Tim.* 47 A; *Soph.* 234 D.

[10] *De post. C.* 126; *Cong.* 143. Cf. *Theaet.* 184 B, C, D.

Philo adopts the Stoic theory at all,[1] it is in the interest of the exaltation of mind as the only active power.

By meditation, the mind can abstract from the data of sense the permanent and abiding elements[2] and from what is seen draw conclusions as to the unseen.[3] Observing, for example, the visible universe and especially the ordered movements of the stars, it reasons to the notion of a God who gives them motion, who cares for them. Philo is never done telling of the excellences of sight. It is the most excellent and dominant of all the outward senses,[4] by far the most precious power we possess,[5] akin to the soul,[6] like the sun,[7] the origin of philosophy.[8] The notion of the perfection and wonder of the faculty of sight and its connection with philosophy through the effect that the sight of the ordered movements of the heavens has on the soul, comes from Plato.[9] Next after sight, though far inferior to it, Philo puts hearing. It is a less trustworthy witness than sight,[10] but it too is among the higher senses,[11] is more detached from the body and so more philosophic than smell, touch, or taste.[12] It is with respect to their function as supplying the data of knowledge that Philo speaks of the senses as aids of the soul and as forming its bodyguard.[13] Even the passions are in a certain sense helpers.[14]

[1] See above, p. 64; *Leg. all.* 1:30.

[2] *Theaet.* 185 C, 186 D. Cf. *De cherub.* 97; *Conf. ling.* 133; *Sp. leg.* 1:20, 37; *Quod det. pot.* 86–90.

[3] *Theaet.* 186 D; *Phaedr.* 249 B; *Tim.* 47 B f. Cf. *De Ab.* 162; *Leg. all.* 3:97 f.; *Quod det. pot.* 86; *Conf. ling.* 98; *De sac. A. et C.* 95.

[4] *De Ab.* 57, 60; *Fug. et Inv.* 208; *Conf. ling.* 57, 140, 148; *Sp. leg.* 3:184, 195, 202; *De sac. A. et C.* 78.

[5] *De eb.* 154; *Sp. leg.* 1:29, 4:157; *Vit. cont.* 10; *Quaes. in Gen.* 1:39; *V.M.* 1:124.

[6] *De Ab.* 150–55; *Sp. leg.* 3:192–94.

[7] *Quod Deus sit* 79. [8] *De Ab.* 160–66 and note 2 above.

[9] *Phaedr.* 250 D; *Tim.* 47 A f.; *Rep.* 507 C.

[10] *De Ab.* 60, 150; *Decal.* 35; *Conf. ling.* 57, 140 f., 148; *Sp. leg.* 4:60 f., 137; *De eb.* 82; *Fug. et Inv.* 208; *Mut. nom.* 102; *V.M.* 1:274. Cf. *Theaet.* 201 B.

[11] *Sp. leg.* 1:29, 193, 338–43; *V.M.* 2:211; Cf. Plato *Phil.* 51 B–E.

[12] *De Ab.* 147–50, 241.

[13] *V.M.* 2:81; *Leg. all.* 2:5–8. For the senses as bodyguard see *Somn.* 1:27 and p. 95 below.

[14] *Leg. all.* 2:9 f. Bréhier (*Allegories*), in his note on this passage accuses Philo of inconsistency in calling the passions βοηθοί. But Philo says in § 10 οὐ κυρίως δὲ οὗτοι βοηθοί ἀλλὰ καταχρηστικῶς λέγονται.

There are many points in which Philo repeats Plato. The mind is the eye of the soul.[1] By it we become aware of the ideas, the permanent and unchanging things whose imperfect copies appear in the changing flux of visible, corporeal existence.[2] Now while the mind is engaged in this reflection on its own experience, in the effort, that is, to compare and relate the multitude of particulars, the activity of the senses is distracting. The mind can best accomplish its own special work in abstraction from the outward senses.[3] Moreover the conclusions of the mind have a higher truth than the disordered reports of the senses.[4] The general principles, the categories by which we know, are not given by the senses.[5] In this effort of thought the mind reaches the comprehension of the true realities. But the knowledge thus attained is weak and partial, full of error,[6] subject to change and revision.[7] The ultimate nature of being we do not know.[8] Only human analogies can be used and we have to recognize their inadequacy.[9]

The freedom for the speculative instinct Plato gets partly by the use of myth and partly by allegorical interpretation of the poets.[10] Philo secures it through the allegorical interpretation of the Old Testament. The doctrine of inspiration on which this is based can be paralleled in

---

[1] Suggested in Plato *Symp.* 219 A, 212 A; *Phaedo* 83 B, 99 D E, 66 E. The phrase occurs in Arist. *Eth. Nic.* 1144 a 30; cf. 1096 b 29. Cf. Philo *Mig. Ab.* 39, 49, 77, 165, 191, 222; *De op. mund.* 53, 71; *De plant.* 21 f., 58, 169; *De eb.* 44, 108; *Quod Deus sit* 45; *De sob.* 3, 4, 5; *Conf. ling.* 92; *Cong.* 47, 135; *Somn.* 1:117, 164, 199; 2:160, 171; *Quis rer. div.* 89; *Mut. nom.* 3, 5, 203; *De Ab.* 57, 70; *Jos.* 106; *V.M.* 1:185, 289; 2:51; *Decal.* 68; *Sp. leg.* 1:37, 49, 259; 3:2, 4, 6; 4:140; *De praem.* 37 1.; *De virt.* 11 f., 151; *Vit. cont.* 10; *Leg. ad Gai.* 2, 109; *Mund.* 5 (M. 607); *Frg.* in M. 636; M. 665–66, 672.

[2] *Symp.* 211 B, 247 D, 250 C. Cf. Philo *De praem.* 28 f.; *De plant.* 50; *De eb.* 70, 99, 124, 132 f.; *Quod det. pot.* 75 ff.; *Quis. rer. div.* 280; *Sp. leg.* 1:327–29; *Quaes. in Gen.* 1:54.

[3] *Phaedo* 65 B C; *Quis. rer. div.* 84, 257; *Mig. Ab.* 190–204; *Jos.* 142; *Quaes. in Gen.* 124; *Sp. leg.* 1:298; 4:114 f.; *Somn.* 1:43, 79, 84.

[4] *Quis rer. div.* 71; *De eb.* 170 f., 185–92; *De cherub.* 65 f., 70; *Conf. ling.* 52 f., 92; Plato *Theaet.* 157 E, 185 D E; Zeller, *Stoics, Epicureans, and Skeptics*, p. 91, n. 2.

[5] *Theaet.* 185 A–186 A. Cf. *De cherub.* 97.

[6] *Phaedo* 85 C; *Tim.* 29 C D; Philo *Frg.* in M. 626, 662; *De op. mund.* 5 f.; *Quaes. in Gen.* 1:11; *De post. C.* 152; *De plant.* 80 ff.; *Somn.* 1:6–10.

[7] *De aet. m.* 59.

[8] See above, pp. 17 ff., with notes.

[9] See above, pp. 18 ff., notes 3 and 4 on p. 19.

[10] See Shorey, *Unity*, p. 35 with notes. Hersiman, *Greek Allegorical Interpretation*, p. 8. Allegorical interpretation is playful in Plato.

Plato. The poet, the philosopher, the law-giver, the prophet and the rhapsode all act, according to Plato, under the influence of divine inspiration.[1] This renders them incapable of themselves knowing what they say.[2] The work produced under the influence of inspiration is at times half playfully taken as a source from which we may get truth inaccessible to ordinary human thought.[3] The poets speak in riddles and have to be interpreted in the light of truths we know.[4] So in Philo, not only the writers of the Old Testament[5] but the philosopher, the prophet and the law-giver[6] are regarded as inspired. Philo has himself had the experience a countless number of times.[7] Work done under such inspiration contains truth beyond the reach of the unaided human mind. But this truth is set forth in dark sayings which only those can interpret who are themselves inspired.[8] The inspired speaker or writer is the mere mouthpiece of God and does not himself know what he is saying.[9] The test of an interpretation of any given passage of Scripture is its accordance with known truth,[10] and many interpretations are possible for a given passage.[11] Philo is sufficiently true to the traditions of his race to make full use of the opportunity this theory affords of making Moses the source of Greek thought,[12] and he glorifies the Law in language that indicates the reverence that, as a loyal Jew, he felt for the divine oracles.[13]

It is frequently stated by students of Philo that this doctrine of inspiration is new. Contrasts are drawn between his mysticism and

[1] For the poets see *Phaedr.* 245 A, 265 B; *Ion.* 533 C–534 E; *Apol.* 22 A–C; *Laws* 682 A, 719 C; *Meno* 81 A B, 99 D. For the philosopher see *Phaedr.* 249 C D. For the law-giver see *Meno* 99 D; cf. *Phaedr.* 244 B. For the prophet see *Meno* 99 C D; cf. *Phaedr.* 244. For the rhapsode see *Ion* 536, 542.

[2] *Meno* 99 C; *Ion* 534 C D.

[3] *Meno* 81 B; *Theaet.* 194 C.

[4] *Rep.* 332 B, ᾐνίξατο. Cf. *Theaet.* 194 C and the interpretation of Simonides in *Prot.* 339 A–347 A.

[5] *Passim.* See especially on the translators *V.M.* 2:37 f.

[6] Philosopher, *Decal.* 35; *Fug. et Inv.* 168 f.; *Mut nom.* 39, 136; *De post. C.* 157; *Mig. Ab.* 34 f.; *De sob.* 27; *Somn.* 2:232; *Quis rer. div.* 69 f., 249; *De plant.* 39; *De eb.* 99, 147 ff.; *Sp. leg.* 3:1. Prophet, *Sp. leg.* 1:65, 315; 4:49, 192; *V.M.* 1:57, 175, 277, 283, 286, 288; 2:6, 265, 272; *Somn.* 2:172. Law-giver, *Decal.* 175; *Cong.* 132.

[7] *Mig. Ab.* 34 f.; cf. *Sp. leg.* 3:1.   [10] *Quod det. pot.* 13; *De post. C.* 1–4.
[8] *Mig. Ab.* 84.   [11] *Conf. ling.* 190 f.; *Leg. all.* 1:59.
[9] *Ibid.* 35.   [12] *Quis rer. div.* 214; cf. *V.M.* 2:3

[13] *Mig. Ab.* 60–62, 90–94; *Somn.* 2:123–32; *Decal.* 96–101; *Sp. leg.* 1:31, 315–18; *Jos.* 42 f.; *V.M.* 2:12–36.

the Greek emphasis on reason and its powers.[1] Such contrasts are due to the fact that, for the moment at least, the mystic elements in Plato have been overlooked. Plato recognized the limitations of the human intellect and professes to give only a probable account of things beyond its grasp.[2] He, in some moods, makes the highest knowledge come to men when their minds are passive.[3] It is a mistake to say, as Professor Brett does,[4] that the idea of a superhuman being in immediate contact with man was foreign to the nature of the Greek. The researches of Rohde[5] have shown us just how familiar this conception was to the Greek mystic. Plato himself is influenced by it in his mythology, for example, of Eros.[6] It is necessary to remember, too, that the great emphasis put upon the theory of divine illumination in Philo is, in part at least, due to the fact that his work takes the form very largely of the interpretation of a divinely inspired book. The place that the vision of God has in Philo's system can be better treated in connection with his ethical theory. Enough has been said here to show that Philo's teaching on the subject of knowledge is not a confused mixture of irreconcilable theories[7] but is in striking accord with Plato's recognition of the limits of human thought and of the right and duty of thinkers to give a probable account of the universe. To be probable, Plato believed that such an account must support the faith which he regarded as fundamental, the faith, that is to say, in the coincidence of virtue and happiness[8] and in the value of study and contemplation.[9] Only a rigid, mechanical interpretation can find inconsistency between such a view of the place of divine inspiration in philosophy and the doctrine of the supremacy of the mind emphasized so persistently in Philo's teaching.

Thus far the senses have been dealt with in their relation to thought. They must next be treated in connection with their relation to the will, in the aspect, that is, in which they give rise to impulse and desire. The ὁρμαί must be checked by reason.[10] From excessive ὁρμαί come ἐπι-

---

[1] See Brett, *History of Psychology*, pp. 248 ff.; Bréhier, *Id. phil. et relig.*, p. 200; M. Apelt, "De rationibus quibusdam," etc., p. 112–15 (in *Comm. Phil. Jen.*, Vol. VIII).

[2] See above, p. 19, notes 3 and 4.

[4] *History of Psychology*, p. 248.

[3] See above, p. 67, n. 2.

[5] *Psyche*, II, 14 ff.

[6] *Symp.* 202 E f.; cf. *Ion.* 533 E; *Phaedr.* 253 A.

[7] M. Apelt (*op. cit.*, p. 115) calls Philo's teaching a "decretorum confusio."

[8] Cf. *Rep.* 618 E; *Gorg.* 509 A; *Laws* 662 B; and Shorey, *Unity*, p. 25.

[9] Cf. *Meno* 86 B, 81 D; *Phaedo* 89 D–91 C.

[10] *Sp. leg.* 2:142, 163; 4:79.

θυμίαι.¹ It is because of this relationship to passion that αἴσθησις is condemned.² Plato's polemic against the senses has the same basis.³ In *Timaeus* 69 D, he speaks of "the mortal part of the soul which has in it dread passions, first pleasure, the greatest bait of evil, next griefs, avoidances of good, then foolhardiness and fear, foolish counsellors, spirit, hard to persuade, and hope that is easily led. These the creative powers mingled with unreasoning αἴσθησις and fashioned the mortal species under the impulse of necessity." Philo's constant use of ἡδονὴ δελέαρ or phrases which echo it shows that this passage was much in his mind.⁴ Even sight and hearing, which are the cause of many blessings, may still, he thinks, be the instruments by which the soul is allured into error. Sight gives to passion the images of pleasure.⁵ Both these senses may be overcome and allured by poetry and art into a false notion of God.⁶ The senses pay tribute to the passions.⁷

The soul incarnate is described, in language echoing that of Plato, as in a prison.⁸ The passage in *Timaeus* 43 A f. has had a great influence on his language. There the body is compared to a river. The revolutions of the immortal soul, bound in this river, βίᾳ δὲ ἐφέροντο καὶ ἔφερον, ὥστε τὸ μὲν ὅλον κινεῖσθαι ζῷον, ἀτάκτως μὴν ὅπῃ τύχοι προιέναι καὶ ἀλόγως, τὰς ἐξ ἁπάσας κινήσεις ἔχον . . . . πολλοῦ γὰρ ὄντος τοῦ κατακλύζοντος καὶ ἀπορρέοντος κύματος ὃ τὴν τροφὴν παρεῖχεν, ἔτι μείζω θόρυβον ἀπηργάζετο τὰ τῶν προσπιπτόντων παθήματα ἑκάστοις, ὅτε πυρὶ προσκρούσειε τὸ σῶμά τινος ἔξωθεν ἀλλοτρίῳ περιτυχὸν . . . . καὶ ὑπὸ πάντων τούτων διὰ τοῦ σώματος αἱ κινήσεις ἐπὶ τὴν ψυχὴν φερόμεναι προσπίπτοιεν . . . . καὶ δὴ καὶ τότε ἐν τῷ παρόντι πλείστην καὶ μεγίστην παρεχόμεναι κίνησιν, μετὰ τοῦ ῥέοντος ἐνδελεχῶς ὀχετοῦ κινοῦσαι καὶ σφοδρῶς σείουσαι τὰς τῆς ψυχῆς περιόδους, τὴν μὲν ταὐτοῦ παντάπασιν ἐπέδησαν ἐνάντια αὐτῇ ῥέουσαι. There are many reminiscences of the language of this passage in

[1] *Quis rer. div.* 245; *Cong.* 60.

[2] *Leg. all.* 3:220 f.; *Mig. Ab.* 204; *De Ab.* 236–40; *Quis rer. div.* 52; *Somn.* 1:246; 2:267.

[3] *Phaedo* 69 A ff.; *Prot.* 352 D f.; *Phaedr.* 258 E.

[4] See *De ag.* 103; *V.M.* 1:295; *De eb.* 70, 165; *De sob.* 23; *Mig. Ab.* 29, 150; *Quis rer. div.* 71; *Mut. nom.* 172; *Cong.* 77; *De post. C.* 72; *Quod Deus sit* 115, 168; *De virt.* 36; *et al.*

[5] *De praem.* 19.   [6] *Sp. leg.* 1:29.

[7] *De Ab.* 236–40, 243 f.; *Quis rer. div.* 186.

[8] See *Phaedo* 62 B, 67 D, 82 E, 114 B; *Phaedr.* 250 C. Compare in Philo *Quis rer. div.* 68, 85, 109, 273; *Mut. nom.* 173; *Somn.* 1:139, 181; *Quod Deus sit* 111 ff.; *De eb.* 101; *Mig. Ab.* 9.

Philo. The parallel in *De gig.* 13 has already been quoted[1] in connection with Philo's teaching on the descent and ascent of souls. Others follow.

δικαίῳ ὃς οὐ παρεσύρη τῇ τοῦ κατακλυσμοῦ φορᾷ [*Quod det. pot.* 170].

τὴν τῶν αἰσθητῶν φυρὰν ποταμοῦ πλημμυροῦντος δίκην ἐπιχεῖσθαι, μηδενὸς τὴν βίαιον ὁρμὴν ἀνωθοῦντος· τότε γὰρ ἐγκαταποθεὶς ὁ νοῦς τοσούτῳ κλύδωνι βύθιος εὑρίσκεται, μηδ' ὅσον ἀνανήξασθαι καὶ ὑπερκύψαι δυνάμενος [*Quod det. pot.* 100].

πολλῷ τῷ τῆς ἀφροσύνης χρησάμενος ῥεύματι ἐπικλυσθεὶς κατεπόθη [*Quod Deus sit* 181].

τὰς δὲ ψυχὰς ποταμοῦ χειμάρρου τρόπον ἀμετρίᾳ τροφῶν ἐπικλύζοντες [*De eb.* 22].

ἵνα τοῖς ἐπιρρέουσιν αἰσθητοῖς καταλυζομένη μηδέποτε πρὸς οὐρανὸν ἀνακύψῃ [*De eb.* 70].

It is unnecessary to quote other passages in full. The figure is found in *Conf. ling.* 23, 105; *Fug. et Inv.* 49, 91; *Mut. nom.* 186, 214, 239; *Somn.* 2:109; *Sp. leg.* 2:147; and elsewhere.

Naturally and of necessity, then, man is, according to Philo, oppressed by passion, imperfect and enslaved.[2] To be completely sinless is a special prerogative of God.[3] The best that man can hope to do is to incline somewhat toward the better elements within him, but even this he cannot do all his life.[4] In spite of lofty professions we see men overcome by the false attraction of worldly goods.[5] Even a perfect man, since he is mortal, cannot escape sin.[6] The rational movements of the senses must be ascribed to God, the irrational to the senses themselves, led astray by sensible objects.[7] In other passages, Philo says that all activities of our mind and sense are to be ascribed to God.[8] Moreover God is the cause of all moral progress. It is fatal to think that the credit for any advance can be taken to one's self.[9]

---

[1] See above, p. 43.

[2] *Quis rer. div.* 272–75; cf. *Fug. et Inv.* 104 f.

[3] *De virt.* 177.

[4] *Mut. nom.* 185–87.

[5] *De eb.* 56–63; *Mig. Ab.* 172.

[6] *Sp. leg.* 1:252. But compare *Sp. leg.* 3:134 f. where we are told that the High Priest may escape both voluntary and involuntary sin and that private persons may escape voluntary sin.

[7] *De sac. A. et C.* 106.

[8] *Mut. nom.* 56, 155, 220 f.; *Cong.* 96 f., 130; *Somn.* 2:290; *Fug. et Inv.* 135; *Quis rer. div.* 73 f., 85, 105–8; *Conf. ling.* 124–27; *De sac. A. et C.* 2 ff.; *De post. C.* 175.

[9] *De ag.* 169 ff.; *De sac. A. et C.* 71; *Somn.* 2:24 f.

MAN'S SOUL AND ITS POWERS

Such passages are in flat contradiction to the group in which man's freedom and responsibility are asserted,[1] but this inconsistency is one that Philo shares with most determinists.[2] It is in Plato. In *Laws* 860 ff., Plato seeks to reconcile the conception that injustice is always involuntary with the necessary legal distinction between voluntary and involuntary injustice. An action is voluntary, he says, ἐὰν ἤθει καὶ δικαίῳ τρόπῳ χρώμενός τις ὠφελῇ τινά τι καὶ βλάπτῃ (862 B). The unjust man must be punished. Punishment is remedial if the disease of the soul is curable.[3] It is verbally inconsistent with both his determinism and his doctrine of the freedom and responsibility of all men for Philo to maintain the Stoic paradox that the wise man is free, while the man who follows his senses is bound to the wheel of necessity.[4] But this inconsistency is one that moral teachers who believe in determinism cannot escape. We may note in this connection the contrast between the determinism of *Timaeus* (86 D ff.), and Plato's inspirational utterances, of which ἀρετὴ δὲ ἀδέσποτον (*Rep.* 617 E) is the type.[5] There is a similar inconsistency in Stoicism.[6]

[1] Cf. *Quod Deus sit* 45–50; *De mund.* 5 (M. 607); *Frg.* in M. 660; *Quod det. pot.* 11; *De gig.* 47; *Quaes. in Gen.* 1:21.

[2] See Shorey in *AJP*, X, 77.

[3] *Gorg.* 477 A–478 E, 505 B; *Prot.* 324 B, 325 D, 326 D E. Cf. in Philo *De sob.* 23; *Conf. ling.* 181; *Quod det. pot.* 143 f.; *De ag.* 40; *De eb.* 28; *Cong.* 157–62, 167, 172, 175, 177–80; *Somn.* 2:294 f.

[4] For the freedom of the wise man see *De sob.* 57; *Fug. et Inv.* 16; *Mig. Ab.* 45; *Quis rer. div.* 275. For the wheel of necessity see *Somn.* 2:44.

[5] For Plato's determinism see Shorey, *Unity*, p. 9, and *AJP*, X, p. 77.

[6] For Stoic fatalism see Zeller, *Stoics, Epicureans, and Skeptics*, pp. 332 f., and contrast with it the doctrine of the freedom of the wise man, *ibid.*, p. 270, n. 3. Freedom here means rational self-determination.

CHAPTER V

ETHICS

In contrast to the life in the body, with its weakness, its temptations, and its distractions, Plato, and Philo with him, imagines the life of the free spirit in the region above sense, where, undisturbed, it enjoys the high pleasures of knowledge,[1] perfect peace,[2] and joy.[3] It is this life of pure contemplation which constitutes the highest good. Platonic phraseology is frequent in Philo's descriptions of this state. He who has attained it is the man who sees God[4] and is His friend.[5] He alone can worship God acceptably since he is free from all impurity.[6] He has been initiated into the great mysteries.[7]

Philo adds to these Platonic phrases another formulation of the same notion which has been regarded as expressing a new idea distinctive of his thought.[8] He uses πίστις in the sense of confidence in God and as practically synonymous with ἐπιστήμη. The place this conception holds in his system is indicated by the eloquent panegyric in *De Ab.* 268.

Faith toward God is the only undeceiving and certain good, the consolation of life, the fulness of good hopes, the banishment of evils, the bringing of blessings, the renunciation of misfortune, the knowledge of piety, the possession of happiness, the bettering in all things of the soul which rests for its support upon Him who is the cause of all things, and who, though He can do all things, wills only to do what is best.[9]

---

[1] Cf. *Phaedr.* 247 D and Philo *De op. mund.* 69–71; *De eb.* 99; *Conf. ling.* 95–97; *Somn.* 1:59 f.

[2] *Fug. et Inv.* 173 f.; *Mig. Ab.* 63; *De gig.* 52; *De eb.* 75, 100.

[3] *Fug. et Inv.* 176; *De plant.* 168; *De eb.* 62; *De Ab.* 202, 205, 207; *Sp. leg.* 2:48, 55.

[4] Plato *Phaedr.* 249 C f. Compare Philo *De praem.* 27; *De eb.* 82, 94, 107, 152; *Quis rer. div.* 36, 78; *Mig. Ab.* 18, 38, 46, 168 f.; *De plant.* 27, 58; 64; *Quod Deus sit* 3; *Conf. ling.* 56; *Quod det. pot.* 158 f.; *De gig.* 53; *Somn.* 2:276, 279; *De Ab.* 79 f.; *Fug. et Inv.* 141, 165.

[5] Plato *Symp.* 212 A; cf. Philo *De eb.* 94; *Frg.* in M. 652.

[6] Plato *Phaedo* 67 B; cf. Philo *V.M.* 2:150; *Frg.* in M. 660.

[7] Plato *Phaedr.* 249 C; cf. Philo *De praem.* 120–25.

[8] Bréhier, *Id. phil. et relig.*, pp. 218 f.

[9] Translation by Hatch, *Essays in Biblical Greek* (Oxford, 1889), pp. 86 f. In the treatment of πίστις I have followed Hatch closely.

ETHICS

In Plato the word has no such meaning. In *Rep.* 601 E, πίστις is opposed to ἐπιστήμη and is practically equivalent to δόξα. Plato also uses it in the sense of proof or argument, that which creates belief.[1] In Aristotle (*Top.* iv. 5. 125 b), πίστις is contrasted with ὑπόληψις or "impression." A man may have an impression and yet not be sure of it, but πίστις implies certainty. Here the meaning approaches ἐπιστήμη. The conviction may come either through the senses or through the reason.[2] This use also occurs in *Top.* i. 1. 100 b. The word in Aristotle has, in addition to those just mentioned, the meaning of good faith or mutual trust.[3] In later Greek philosophy the word is used in this sense.[4] The Stoics use it in the sense of conviction.[5]

In Philo, πίστις means "the intellectual state of mind which is called 'conviction,' blended with the moral state of mind which is called 'trust.'"[6] It is a conviction resulting from a conception of the nature of God. Good men trust God; other men trust their senses and their reason. In *De op. mund.* 45, Philo tells us that God saw ὅτι πιστεύσουσι (οἱ ἄνθρωποι) μᾶλλον τοῖς φαινομένοις ἢ θεῷ σοφιστείαν πρὸ σοφίας θαυμάσαντες. In *Leg. all.* 3:228 f., confidence in God, τῷ θεῷ πεπιστευκέναι, is the best thing, and not confidence τοῖς ἀσαφέσι λογισμοῖς καὶ τοῖς ἀβεβαίοις εἰκασίαις. True δόγμα is faith in God, false is faith τοῖς κενοῖς λογισμοῖς.[7] Such faith is a prize to be striven for,[8] and is spoken of as the chief of the virtues.[9]

The opposite spirit is called by Philo οἴησις, τῦφος, κενὴ δόξα, ἀφροσύνη, φιλαυτία,[10] and is described in various metaphors.[11] It consists in giving

---

[1] *Phaedo* 70 B, and elsewhere.   [2] *Phys. Auscult.* viii. 8. 262 a.

[3] *Pol.* v. 11. 1313 b, ἡ γὰρ γνῶσις πίστιν ποιεῖ . . . . πρὸς ἀλλήλους.

[4] See *Ethic. Eudem.* vii. 2. 1237 b, οὐκ ἔστι δ' ἄνευ πίστεως φιλία βέβαιος, and pseudo-Aristotle, *De virt. et vit.* 1250 b, ἀκολουθεῖ δὲ τῇ δικαιοσύνῃ . . . . ἡ πίστις καὶ ἡ μισοπονηρία.

[5] Arnim, *Frg.*, III, 147, 10 f.   [6] Hatch, *op. cit.*, p. 84.

[7] § 229. Cf. *Quis. rer div.* 91–93; *Mig. Ab.* 43 f.

[8] *Mig. Ab.* 44; *De praem.* 27, 30.

[9] *Quis rer. div.* 91; *De Ab.* 268; *De cherub.* 85.

[10] οἴησις, *Mut. nom.* 176, same as τῦφος in *Mut. nom.* 103; cf. οἴησις and δόξα in *Sp. leg.* 1:10 f. For a lengthy discussion of κενὴ δόξα, see *Somn.* 2:48–66. It is called ψευδὴς δόξα in *Somn.* 1:218. Cf. ἀφροσύνη in *Somn.* 2:162, 192, 198, 200; φιλαυτία, *Quis rer. div.* 106. Its victim is δοκησίσοφος, *De eb.* 37; *Mut. nom.* 105, 176; *Somn.* 2:298.

[11] Blindness, *Quis rer. div.* 77; *Mig. Ab.* 38. Death, *Quis rer. div.* 201, 291. Banishment, *Cong.* 57; cf. *De cherub.* 121; *Quis rer. div.* 179; *De gig.* 67. Slavery, *De cherub.* 73 f.; *Quod omnis prob. lib.* 11.

to the senses or to the thoughts that are based on them that trust which should be bestowed upon God alone.[1] It is, in other words, the spirit of the materialist who refuses to recognize the supreme reality of the things of the spirit.[2] It may take the form of that prideful spirit which attributes to its own powers alone the knowledge and virtue it possesses and fails to recognize its dependence on God.[3]

The word οἴησις is used frequently in Plato as the equivalent of δόξα, and just as δόξα is to be distinguished from clear knowledge, so οἴησις is used with a derogatory meaning.[4] In Heraclitus, however, we find the word already used in a sense corresponding to the familiar οἴεσθαί τι εἶναι, and meaning self-conceit.[5] In this sense the word passed into later moral philosophy.[6] Philo seems to combine these two meanings. οἴησις is that prideful spirit which is manifested in the δόξα that there is nothing higher than the external world of the senses or than the mind of man.[7] δόξα, just as in Plato,[8] is the mental attitude which corresponds to the sensible world.

The noun τῦφος seems originally to have meant smoke or vapor.[9] It is used by the comedians in the sense of conceit or vanity, probably because this temper clouds or darkens a man's intellect.[10] The word is frequent in late Greek prose.[11] The comic and colloquial associations of the noun are seen also in the early use of the verb τυφόω, especially the perfect passive. The passage in Plato, *Hippias Major* 290 A, illustrates the use. The interlocutor whom Socrates represents asks questions μάλα ὑβριστικῶς (286 C) and the style of the questions is consistently rude and colloquial. Ὦ τετυφωμένε σύ is a rude form of address. So in *Phaedrus* 230 A ἐπιτεθυμμένον, from τύφω, a by-form of τυφόω,

---

[1] *De virt.* 7; *De eb.* 73; *Somn.* 1:77, 118 f.; *Somn.* 2:69, 70, 93–99, 193 f., 290.

[2] *Mig. Ab.* 19, 21; *Quis rer. div.* 71; *Mut. nom.* 205; *De Ab.* 73; *De sob.* 15.

[3] *Sp. leg.* 1:334–36; *De praem.* 13; *De sac. A. et C.* 2 f.; *De post. C.* 175; *Conf. ling.* 124–27; *Mut. nom.* 205; *Somn.* 1:77.

[4] See *Phaedo* 92 A and *Phaedr.* 244 C. So in Aristotle *Rhet. Al.* xv. 4. where οἴησις is opposed to σαφῶς εἰδέναι.

[5] See Diels, *Fragmente d. Vorsokratiker*, p. 68, l. 20, and compare Euripides *Frg.* 644.

[6] Diog. Laert. ix. 7. 4. 50.   [8] *Rep.* 477 A B, 479 D.

[7] See note 3 above.   [9] See Liddell and Scott, *Lexicon*, under τῦφος.

[10] So in Antiphanes (Meineke, *Com. Frag.* III, 328); Menander Ἱππ. 1:7; quoted by Liddell and Scott under τῦφος.

[11] See Plut. 2.81 C E and M. Anton. 2.17; 6.13 (Gataker); quoted by Liddell and Scott, under τῦφος.

ETHICS

is humorous in effect.¹ The word is used of drunkenness in Aristotle, *Problem*. iii. 16. From such associations it passes into the language of moral philosophy in the sense of self-conceit.² In Philo it is a synonym of οἴησις.

What these expressions emphasize is Philo's conviction that only by recognizing the fleetingness and the weakness of all that is human, even of our minds, and by becoming at the same time conscious of the reality that is behind all material existence, can we rise above sense and its distractions and become free. This is Plato's teaching. "God," Plato tells us in *Laws* 803 C, "is the natural and worthy object of our most serious and blessed endeavours, for man, as we said before, is made to be the plaything of God, and this, truly considered, is the best of him."³ Man is a possession belonging to God.⁴ God is the cause of all his activities⁵ and man must use all his powers in pleasing God.⁶

There are many reminiscences of Plato's language in Philo's utterances on this theme.

PLATO:	PHILO:
Phaedr. 249 C: ἐξιστάμενος δὲ τῶν ἀνθρωπίνων σπουδασμάτων καὶ πρὸς τῷ θείῳ γιγνόμενος.	*Fug. et Inv.* 131: τὰς μὲν ἡμετέρας σπουδὰς ἐκλιπόντες, μετοικισάμενοι δ' εἰς τὸν ἔρημον κακῶν εὐσεβῶν χῶρον.
Laws 803 B: τὰ τῶν ἀνθρώπων πράγματα μεγάλης σπουδῆς οὐκ ἄξια.	*Somn.* 2:70: τὰς καταγελάστους τοῦ θνητοῦ βίου σπουδάς.
Ibid. 803 D: τὰς σπουδὰς οἴονται δεῖν ἕνεκα τῶν παιδιῶν γίγνεσθαι.	
Ibid. 803 D: τὰ γὰρ περὶ τὸν πόλεμον . . . . σπουδαῖα ὄντα τῆς εἰρήνης ἕνεκα.	*De eb.* 62: τὰς ἀνθρώπων . . . . σπουδάς, ὅσαι περὶ τῶν κατὰ πόλεμον ἢ κατ' εἰρήνην πραγμάτων εἰσίν.

¹ Cf. Aristophanes *Lysist.* 221; *Demos.* 116. 6; οὐ δὴ ποιήσω τοῦτο· οὐχ οὕτω τετύφωμαι, *Demos.* 229.1; 749.16.

² See examples in Stephanus, *Thesaurus*, under τῦφος. He mentions Diog. Laert. vi. 26; Plutarch. *Moral.* 580 C; *Pericles* c. 5.

³ Cf. also παίγνιον ἐκείνων in *Laws* 644 D. See *Phaedo* 62 B.

⁴ *Phaedo* 62 B; *Laws* 902 B. Cf. *V.M.* 1:157; *De sac. A. et C.* 97; *Sp. leg.* 1:294; *De cherub.* 117 f.

⁵ Plato *Laws* 644 D E. Cf. Philo *Leg. all.* 2:68 f.; *Cong.* 130; *Mut. nom.* 205, 221; *Somn.* 1:244, 2:24 f, 69, 76; *Fug. et Inv.* 135; *Quis rer. div.* 73 f., 105-11; *De sac. A. et C.* 2 ff.; *De post. C.* 175; *Quod Deus sit* 5; *De plant.* 61; *Conf. ling.* 124-27; *Sp. leg.* 1:334-36; *De praem.* 13.

⁶ Plato *Laws* 803 C, *Phaedr.* 249 C. Cf. Philo *Frg.* in M. 660; *Decal.* 37 (καταπειθὴς θεῷ); also *Cong.* 103-6.

For further illustrations of this feeling see *Somn.* 2:133–38; *De eb.* 152; *Conf. ling.* 93; *Mig. Ab.* 20, 32.

Philo has been contrasted with Plato on the ground that the ideal world, the contemplation of which is the perfect life, is for Philo a world of moral ideas only.[1] It does not consist of thoughts hypostatized and made objective, but in the moral conscience. It is external to us because different, and yet internal, united to our soul. But the intelligible world of Philo is not merely "un monde moral"[2] and the ideas of Plato are not merely "pensée condensée," if we are to understand this as not including the high moral concepts. In both authors the world of ideas is a world of concepts made objective, including, besides moral and intellectual notions, the ideal counterparts of all things.[3] It is not identical with the moral consciousness in Philo. In him as in Plato the ideas of high moral concepts enter into the human mind as regulative ideals, but they also remain exterior and objective.[4]

Again, it is said that Philo differs from Plato in that he finds the principle of morality not in nature but in withdrawal into the inner life.[5] But for Plato too the perfect life is the life of contemplation in which the sage retires into himself.[6] This conception does not in Philo, any more than in Plato, displace the ideal of divine harmony which finds the principles of morality in the nature itself. Both in certain moods recognize that the ideal is separation from the body,[7] the negation of the fleshly lusts. But they also in other moods recognize that for men here in this life the ideal is the health and harmony of the powers of the soul.[8] The principle of morality is to this extent in the nature itself. The inconsistency that is here involved is not due to the fact that Philo has adopted the Stoic ideal of complete independence of externals as the ideal for the sage and the Peripatetic ideal for men at a lower stage.[9]

---

[1] Bréhier, *Id. phil. et relig.*, pp. 296 f.
[2] See *Sp. leg.* 1:45–49.
[3] See above, p. 38, with notes 2 and 3.
[4] See above, pp. 37, 38.
[5] Bréhier, *op. cit.*, p. 296.
[6] *Phaedo* 64 E–66 B; *Theaet.* 173 E.
[7] *Phaedo* 64 A–D, 67 E; cf. *De gig.* 14, and see above, pp. 42–43; *Theaet.* 176 A B.
[8] *Mig. Ab.* 104, 119, 155; *De eb.* 140 f.; *De Ab.* 48, 275; *Leg. all.* 3:222 f.; *Frg.* in M. 674; cf. Plato *Gorg.* 504 B–D; *Rep.* 444 D E; 571 D E; 591 B–D.
[9] There is no warrant in *Mig. Ab.* 146 f. for Bréhier's remark (*Id. phil. et relig.*, p. 261), that virtue in the Peripatetic sense, since it is always in danger of falling into one or other of the opposing vices, is that which suits the unstable man. The mean is there "the royal road which God, the only king, has found as the fairest place of sojourning for souls that love virtue." There is no hint that the Peripatetic ideal of virtue belongs to a lower stage. The doctrine of virtue as a mean occurs also in *Fug. et Inv.* 29; *De eb.* 115 f.; *Sp. leg.* 4:102, 168; *Quod Deus sit* 162 ff. Bréhier is led into this mistake by his identification of the Peripatetic ideal with the "political man." The identification cannot hold; see pp. 78 f. below.

ETHICS

We may find a similar blending of "Stoic" and "Peripatetic" ideals in Plato. No inspirational moral teacher can fail to assert man's complete independence of all external goods. These are for Plato merely "so-called goods."[1] But, for common sense, they are really in a mean between the two, capable of causing great evils or of doing us real good.[2] Even the goods of the mind, such, for example, as a quick and ready perception, are good only if directed to good ends.[3] At other times, these bodily and external goods are conventionally adopted as real goods.[4] It is just so in Philo. The rejection of the bodily and external goods is complete,[5] yet they are in common-sense fashion recognized as good if rightly used,[6] and even at times spoken of as good in the conventional, careless language of ordinary folk.[7] As an inspirational teacher Philo refuses to recognize that they are indispensable. He specifically refers to the "comfortable doctrine" of the Peripatetics, but in the spirit of Plato, and not really adopting it as his own.[8]

Philo's language does not warrant, either, the notion that he has adopted the Peripatetic definition of the virtues as means and combined this in an external way with the Stoic definitions which are inconsistent with the Peripatetic point of view. In the longest passage on the subject of the virtues as means,[9] the virtues chosen as examples are defined in language which, as has been pointed out, is parallel with that of the Stoics.[10] The virtues chosen are courage and piety. The definition of courage is, it is true, that of Chrysippus, but the Stoic has drawn from Plato. The close connection of the three authors in ideas and phraseology is obvious when the passages are set side by side.

[1] τὰ λεγόμενα ἀγαθά, *Rep.* 491 C, 495 A; *Charm.* 158 A.

[2] Cf. τὰ μέσα in *Protag.* 346 D, 351 D and see *Lach.* 195 E–196 A; *Charm.* 174 C; *Euthyd.* 292 B; *Phil.* 20 D; *Meno* 88 A.

[3] *Rep.* 519 A; *Laws* 689 C D; *Theaet.* 176 C. Cf. in Philo *De post. C.* 79–81.

[4] *Meno* 78 C D; *Euthyd.* 279 A B; *Gorg.* 467 E.

[5] *Mut. nom.* 173 f., 214 f.; *Fug. et Inv.* 25, 148, 153; *Quis rer. div.* 92; *Cong.* 27; *De gig.* 15; *Conf. ling.* 112, 145; *Mig. Ab.* 145; *Quod det. pot.* 9, 136, 158; *De post. C.* 116 f., 163; *De eb.* 75; *Frg.* in M. 636, 638; *De mund.* (M. 605); *De virt.* 15, 85, 187–89; *De praem.* 24; *Sp. leg.* 1:311; 2:23, 46, 48; 4:80, 82. The list might be multiplied indefinitely.

[6] *De sob.* 38 f.; *Fug. et Inv.* 27–32; *Quaes. in Gen.* 4:121; *Quis rer. div.* 255 f.; *Cong.* 33; *Conf. ling.* 16–20.

[7] *Mig. Ab.* 94, 101; *De eb.* 200–202; *De praem.* 98–105, 118–20; *De virt.* 176; *De Ab.* 219; *Mut. nom.* 221.

[8] *Mig. Ab.* 147, τὴν ἥμερον καὶ κοινωνικὴν .... φιλοσοφίαν. Note the τινες, disclaiming responsibility on his own account and compare *eis* in *Quaes. in Gen.* 4:121. So *Quod det. pot.* 7 ff.

[9] *Sp. leg.* 4:143–48.   [10] Bréhier, *Id. phil. et relig.*, p. 260.

Plato *Laches* 195 A: (ἀνδρείαν) τὴν τῶν δεινῶν καὶ θαρραλέων ἐπιστήμην καὶ ἐν πολέμῳ καὶ ἐν τοῖς ἄλλοις ἅπασιν.

Cf. *Laches* 195 D: τῷ τῶν δεινῶν καὶ μὴ δεινῶν ἐπιστήμονι, ὃν ἐγὼ ἀνδρεῖον καλῶ.

Laches 192 D: ἡ φρόνιμος ἄρα καρτερία . . . . ἀνδρεία ἂν εἴη.

Rep. 430 B: τὴν δὴ τοιαύτην δύναμιν καὶ σωτηρίαν διὰ παντὸς δόξης ὀρθῆς τε καὶ νομίμου δεινῶν τε πέρι καὶ μὴ ἀνδρείαν ἔγωγε καλῶ.

Chrysippus: Fortitudo est, inquit (Chrysippus), scientia rerum perferendarum vel affectio animi in patiendo summae legi parens sine timore (Cicero *Tusc. Disp.* iv. 53).

ἀνδρείαν δὲ ἐπιστήμην δεινῶν καὶ οὐ δεινῶν καὶ οὐδετέρων (Arnim, *Frg.* III, 63, l. 28).

Philo *Sp. leg.* 4:145: τὴν ἀνδρείαν, ἀρετὴν περὶ τὰ δεινὰ πραγματευομένην . . . . τῶν ὑπομενετέων οὖσαν ἐπιστήμην.

Leg. all. 1:68: ἐπιστήμη γάρ ἐστιν (ἀνδρεία) ὑπομενετέων καὶ οὐχ ὑπομενετέων καὶ οὐδετέρων.

It is a significant fact that the suggestion for the doctrine of virtues as means is found in the context of the passages here quoted from the *Laches*. See *Laches* 197 B: ἐγὼ δὲ ἀνδρείας μὲν καὶ προμηθίας πάνυ τισὶν ὀλίγοις οἶμαι μετεῖναι, θρασύτητος δὲ καὶ τόλμης καὶ τοῦ ἀφόβου μετὰ ἀπρομηθίας πάνυ πολλοῖς καὶ ἀνδρῶν καὶ γυναικῶν καὶ παίδων καὶ θηρίων. Philo tells us in the context of the passage quoted above that the excess of courage is θρασύτης and its defect δειλία. It is evident that Philo is to all intents and purposes reproducing Plato. The Platonic text is enlarged and expanded with developments that come from Aristotle and the Stoics, but these expansions are naturally suggested by the Platonic text itself. There is no combining of contrary points of view. It is worth noticing that the definition of piety given in this passage of Philo, *Sp. leg.* 4:147, reproduces that of Plato, *Euthyphro* 14 D. Philo speaks of (εὐσέβεια) ἐπιστήμην ἐμποιοῦσα θεραπείας θεοῦ; Plato defines ὁσιότης as ἐπιστήμη αἰτήσεως καὶ δόσεως θεοῖς. Plato was evidently Philo's model throughout the passage.

It is misleading to identify Philo's conception of political virtue with the Peripatetic ideal.[1] The "political man" is from one point of view entirely praiseworthy. He is able to interpret the dream of human life,[2] he is the good judge,[3] the physician of his people,[4] he who must give the practical, ethical precepts that are to guide them.[5] Like a kindly

[1] Bréhier, *Id. phil. et relig.*, p. 261.
[2] *De Jos.* 125, 143.
[3] *Ibid.* 72 f.
[4] *Ibid.* 32, 33.
[5] *Ibid.* 143 f.

father, he undertakes the care of a city.¹ But this activity, worthy as it is, is not the highest. The life of contemplation is better and will be given as a reward to him who successfully fulfils his duties as a guardian of the people.² The resemblances to Plato are obvious. In Plato's *Republic* the guardians must know the Idea of Good and must mold the people in accordance with it.³ The aim of the political art is to make the citizens better.⁴ The king must be a disinterested guardian of his people.⁵ The man who has the training that would fit him to be a guardian recognizes that the life of contemplation is higher and better, and can only be induced to undertake the necessary work of ruling because of his fear that he may be ruled by an inferior.⁶

But besides this favorable treatment of the political life, mostly confined to the *De Josepho*, there is another which approaches the topic from a different point of view. The political man is the man who values alike the goods of the soul, the body, and the external life. Philo's dualism led him to be suspicious of worldly activity. We have already pointed out that there is in Plato the inconsistency between the inspirational moral teacher and the philosopher who recognizes that human life has to go on in a world where conditions are not ideal.⁷ Philo's treatment of the political man presents a similar inconsistency. Ideally the life of complete withdrawal from the world is best.⁸ But actually the life of the world has its demands. From the latter point of view, the political man who is not overborne by the temptations of such a life is to be praised. But the life is full of temptations and embarrassments to the man who is trying to realize the ideal of the perfectly virtuous life. The political man whom Philo saw in the life about him was one who had been overborne. His descriptions are drawn from two passages of the *Republic*, the passage where the force of public standards is described (492 f.), and the other the account of the democratic man (561). The parallels are so close that it seems worth while to put the passages side by side.

¹ *De Jos.* 67. ² *Fug. et Inv.* 36.

³ *Rep.* 500 D–501 B; *Gorg.* 503 D E; *Pol.* 309 D; *Gorg.* 504 D; *Phaedo* 82 A B. Cf. *Crat.* 389 D and *Rep.* 484 D, 519 D E.

⁴ *Gorg.* 515 C, 516 B.

⁵ Cf. ἐπιμελητής in *Gorg.* 516 B and *Rep.* 345 D, 416 D E, 421 A B.

⁶ *Rep.* 347 C. ⁷ See above, p. 76.

⁸ ἄριστος and ἱερώτατος, *De praem.* 51. Compare *Fug. et Inv.* 36, and Plato *Rep.* 521 A B, 540 B.

Rep. 561 C: τοτὲ μὲν μεθύων καὶ καταυλούμενος.... τοτὲ δ' ὡς ἐν φιλοσοφίᾳ διατρίβων.

Somn. 2:11: οὗτος γὰρ οὐκ ἀλογεῖ μὲν τῶν κατὰ ψυχὴν ἀρετῶν, προμηθεῖται δὲ καὶ τῆς τοῦ σώματος εὐσταθείας.
Mig. Ab. 160 (also of ὁ πολιτευόμενος) ἵνα καὶ τῶν κατὰ σῶμα.... καὶ τῶν κατὰ ψυχήν.... ἐφάπτηται.

Ibid. 561 D: πολλάκις δὲ πολιτεύεται.... κἂν ποτέ τινας πολεμικοὺς ζηλώσῃ, ταύτῃ φέρεται, ἢ χρηματιστικοὺς ἐπὶ τοῦτ' αὖ.

Somn. 2:11: ἀνθέλκεται δὲ εἰκότως πολλὰ τέλη τοῦ βίου προτεθειμένος.
Ibid. 2:12: πολλὴ γάρ ἐστιν ὅτε ῥυεῖσα πρὸς πλοῦτον καὶ δόξαν ὁρμὴ τὰς περὶ σῶμα καὶ ψυχὴν φροντίδας ἐξενίκησεν, εἶτα ἀντιβιασθεῖσα πάλιν ὑπὸ ἀμφοῖν ὑπὸ τῆς ἑτέρας ἐνικήθη.

Rep. 561 D: οὔτε τις τάξις οὔτε ἀνάγκη ἔπεστιν αὐτοῦ τῷ βίῳ.

Somn. 2:11: σείεται καὶ κλονεῖται, μὴ δυνάμενος στηριχθῆναι.
De Jos. 34: πολύμορφον καὶ πολυειδῆ.

Rep. 492 D: τὸν μὴ πειθόμενον ἀτιμίαις τε καὶ χρήμασι καὶ θανάτοις κολάζουσι.

De Jos. 35: δοῦλος.... ἀπαχθεὶς ὑπὸ μυρίων δεσποτῶν, is suggested by *Republic* 492 B ff., the account of the force of public opinion.

The dual point of view which we have seen in connection with the doctrine of the political man is also to be noticed in Philo's treatment of pleasure. Philo is here in complete accord with Plato. In the mood of high moral enthusiasm he denounces pleasure as utterly evil,[1] but in other moods, he recognizes its place in human life. It is described as the cause of activity among men, a princess and a queen.[2] Many pleasures are necessary.[3] To represent the pleasure of the intellect and

[1] *De op. mund.* 79, 164, 166; *De virt.* 36; *De gig.* 40; *De praem.* 117; *Quaes. in Gen.* 1:51; *Leg. all.* 2:107 f.; *Decal.* 122; *De ag.* 103, 105; *Sp. leg.* 2:195. Compare Plato *Phil.* 44 C; *Gorg.* 493 B, D, E; and note καλουμένας in *Phaedo* 64 D.

[2] *De ag.* 22-25; *De eb.* 216; *De op. mund.* 162.

[3] *Leg. all.* 2:17; *V.M.* 1:160; *Decal.* 45; *Sp. leg.* 3:8 f.; *De eb.* 214-19; *Somn.* 2:215; *De sob.* 61. Compare Plato *Phaedo* 64 D; *Phil.* 62 E.

religious ecstasy Philo prefers, not ἡδονή with its low associations, but χαρά or εὐδαιμονία.[1] In this shrinking from the word ἡδονή, Philo is at one with Plato.[2]

The conception of moral progress which we find in Philo, so far from being something new and foreign to Greek thought,[3] is a legitimate development of Plato's moral teaching. The discipline of the guardians in the *Republic* is Philo's model in part, but there are other Platonic sources. The hints in Plato were developed and systematized into a doctrine by the Stoics, and Philo uses their language and ideas freely. These Stoic developments are not, however, inconsistent with Platonism. Philo is at one with both Plato and the Stoics in his conviction that the highest stage of virtue is a disciplined mind with clear insight into the truth and disciplined passions which obey the dictates of reason.[4] This state can be attained, he thinks, by a rigorous training of the will;[5] it may be a natural endowment,[6] or it may come from instruction.[7] Primarily there are three means which must combine to produce virtue. One must have the natural ability to acquire it, and this natural gift must be cultivated by a discipline of the will and by instruction.[8] But Philo seems to think that any one of these by itself may produce virtue.[9] There is a virtue which comes spontaneously, one which comes through discipline of the will, and one which comes through instruction. To express the same idea differently, there are three roads to wisdom, intellectual effort, moral effort, and divine inspiration. But in Philo as in Plato these three are ordinarily factors combining to produce perfect virtue. So, in Plato, the guardians who have the necessary intellectual

---

[1] *De cherub.* 12; *Quaes. in Gen.* 1:56; *De Ab.* 164.

[2] See Shorey, *Unity*, p. 22 and n. 128.

[3] Bréhier, *Id. phil. et relig.*, pp. 251, 309.

[4] Compare *Laws* 689 D; *Rep.* 485, 486, 539 D ff.; *Pol.* 309 A B; Shorey, *Unity*, p. 11. For Stoics see Arnim, *Frg.*, III, 48, ll. 7, 16-19; Zeller, *Stoics, Epicureans, and Skeptics*, pp. 254 ff.; Seneca *Epist.* 89. 8.

[5] *Rep.* 518 B-521 B. Note ἐμποιεῖσθαι ἔθεσι καὶ ἀσκήσεσιν—518 E; *Laws* 647 D E, 653, 659 D E; 807 D; *Rep.* 465. See Musonius on the ἀσκητής in Bréhier, *op. cit.*, p. 267.

[6] *Rep.* 493 A, 520 B, 366 C; *Laws* 642 C D, 951 B; *Meno* 92 E, 99 E. See Shorey, "Idea of Good," *Class. Phil.*, I, 201. Cf. Arnim, *Frg.*, III, 217.

[7] *Rep.* 518 B- 521 B.

[8] *De Ab.* 53, 54; *De sob.* 38; *Leg. all.* 1:95; *Mut. nom.* 212; *V.M.* 1:21-23. Cf. Arist. in Diog. Laert. v. 18; Plato *Rep.* 518 B, 521 B; *Protag.* 323 C; and see Bréhier, *op. cit.*, p. 273.

[9] *De Jos.* 1; *Cong.* 35-38.

endowment are to acquire the moral virtues ἔθεσι καὶ ἀσκήσεσιν and by intellectual discipline are to be developed to insight.[1] The development of the moral and the intellectual sides of the personality must go on simultaneously. At the highest stage intellectual insight and righteousness must both be present.[2]

There is, however, a difference in emphasis in Philo and Plato. Except in a few passages,[3] Plato gives the impression of making the intellect the supreme thing. Morality is only one element in the perfect life and that not the one which is most emphasized. Hard self-discipline in morals could not of itself, in Plato's system, bring man to the contemplation of the true realities. In Philo it can, and this difference shows how Philo valued moral effort in and for itself. He tells us that in the sphere of morals, effort is to be continued regardless of success. The mere effort in itself is worth while.[4] This emphasis on moral effort is in part due to Stoic influence,[5] but Philo's Jewish heritage no doubt helped to produce it.

There are traces of Platonic influence in Philo's description of each of the three types of virtue. The αὐτομαθής, or spontaneously virtuous man, will be first considered. According to one passage this αὐτομαθής is not a man but a "most pure disposition of the mind, good by nature rather than by discipline, composed not of human reasonings but of divine madness."[6] It is thus equivalent to divine inspiration. It is called laughter[7] and is the joy of divine communion.[8] We may compare it with the Platonic ἔρως or θεία μανία.[9] In other passages, the αὐτομαθής is a real being corresponding to the sage who has finally achieved freedom from the body and who sees God without intermediaries.[10] From this point of view, he resembles the gods of the *Phaedrus* who stand outside the world and look at pure being directly.[11]

---

[1] *Rep.* 518 B–521 B. Cf. *Rep.* 444 D and see Shorey, *Unity*, p. 11, with notes.

[2] *Rep.* 485, 486, 539 D; *Pol.* 309 A B. Cf. in Philo *De ag.* 58 f.; *Quis rer. div.* 77; *De praem.* 120–25; *Conf. ling.* 52; *Mut. nom.* 209; *De eb.* 71, 86, 94, 112, 135; *De sac. A. et C.* 26; *Sp. leg.* 1:287, 2:147.

[3] *Laws* 689, 643 D E; *Theaet.* 176 C.

[4] *De sac. A. et C.* 115–17; *De post. C.* 78; *Quod Deus sit* 92 f.

[5] See Bréhier, *op. cit.*, p. 266 f., with references there to Seneca *Epist.* 31. 4 and *Epist.* 75. 8–18; and Musonius (in Stobaeus *Floril.* ii. 13).

[6] *Fug. et Inv.* 167–68. [9] *Symp.* 204 f.; *Phaedr.* 244 ff., especially 256 B.

[7] *De plant.* 168. [10] *De sac. A. et C.* 78 f.; *Cong.* 111 f.; *Conf. ling.* 79–82.

[8] *Mut. nom.* 131 f. [11] *Phaedr.* 247B f.

While the αὐτομαθής is the type of him who attains by grace,[1] yet grace is needed to make instruction and discipline possible. These too are gifts of God. He who thinks that his own will and intellect is the cause of these goods is still bound to becoming.[2] This emphasis on the weakness of man's powers in the sphere of morals is Platonic. The doctrine of Eros in the *Symposium*,[3] the θεία μοῖρα necessary to salvation in the ordinary Greek state of his day,[4] the θεία φύσις which gives men a noble disdain of wrongdoing,[5] suggest, at any rate, the doctrine of salvation by grace. Plato even goes so far as to say that all man's activities come from God.[6]

But the human spirit may escape from its prison house and rise to the contemplation of the true reality in another way. It is the way of crucifying the flesh. The true philosopher according to Plato dies every day he lives. Philo is completely at one with him in this conception. For both thinkers, the philosopher tries to separate himself from sense and the body with their snares and delusions, and live, as far as is possible in this world, the pure life of the spirit.[7] The effort is great. The gods have set toil before virtue.[8] Most men arrive at the state of freedom and insight only by a strenuous mental and moral discipline.[9] But man is not left to make the struggle unaided. Love, the enthusiastic desire for the higher life, leads him on to success.[10] The soul receives a foretaste of the joy of the free spirit and this keeps

[1] *Mut. nom.* 256–58.

[2] *Leg. all.* 3:136 f.; *De ag.* 169–71; and above, p. 74 with n. 3.

[3] *Symp.* 210 f.   [5] *Rep.* 366 C.

[4] *Rep.* 493 A; *Meno* 94 B, 99 C–E; *Laws* 951 B.   [6] *Laws* 644 D E.

[7] Plato *Phaedo* 64 A, 67 E, 80 E; Philo *De gig.* 14; *Quod det. pot.* 27, 34, 48; *Mig. Ab.* 23, 53, 58, 141, 168 f.; *De plant.* 25; *De sac. A. et C.* 6; *Frg.* in M. 654; *Mut. nom.* 34, 209; *Somn.* 2:70.

[8] Plato *Laws* 718 E. Cf. figure of contest in *Rep.* 465 D, 466 A; *Phaedr.* 256 B; praise of toil in Philo *Mut. nom.* 170, 193; *V.M.* 2:183 f.; *Sp. leg.* 2:60; *Frg.* in M. 668; *Mig. Ab.* 220, 221; *Quod det. pot.* 9, 27; *Cong.* 162, 166 f.; *De sac. A. et C.* 35 f., 112–14; figure of contest of virtue in *Mig. Ab.* 26 f., 133 f., 199 f.; *Quis rer. div.* 47; *Fug. et Inv.* 40, 187; *Jos.* 223; *De Ab.* 35, 40, 48; *Mut. nom.* 48, 81–83, 106; *Sp. leg.* 1:38; *De praem.* 5, 6, 52; *De ag.* 119–23; *Leg. all.* 2:108; 3:18, 48, 74.

[9] One aim of the *Republic* is to show how virtue, instead of being a casual product, may be the normal life of every citizen. The guardians achieve the highest virtue. They do so only through the "longer way" of mental and moral discipline described in Book vii. This, as will be shown later, is paralleled by the ἄσκησις and παιδεία of Philo.

[10] For love as the source of virtue see *Somn.* 1:107, 165; *Sp. leg.* 1:50; *De virt.* 55, 120; *De praem.* 38, 84. Cf. Eros in *Symp.* 211 f. and *Phaedr.* 248.

it eager and gives it courage and energy in the struggle against the allurements of sense. Love supplies the motive for the careful ordering of the life, the strenuous moral discipline that will lead to the final conquering of sin.[1] Under its influence, man struggles upward, with many a fall, it is true, but with the chance of ultimate success. This that Philo calls love is the unexplained impulsion of our nature toward good.[2] Philo is in all this teaching at one with Plato, as we have said. His doctrine of love is not an element completely foreign to Greek ethical teaching,[3] but is based on the mystical element which is prominent in Plato. By his resort to myth in his description of Love in the *Symposium* Plato indicates that the impulse toward good is not to be explained on logical grounds, yet this unexplained emotion plays a real part in his system of ethics.[4] It is not in Plato a purely intellectual passion. Some souls, he tells us in the *Phaedrus*, have "had their hearts turned to unrighteousness by some corrupting influence" and do not easily recall the images of the other world.[5] Throughout Plato's teaching the idea of beauty is hardly to be distinguished from the idea of good.[6] In *Laws* 711 D, Plato speaks of "divine love of the temperate and just ways of life." In the *Phaedrus*, he explains it, as Philo often does, as due to divine inspiration.[7]

This impulsion of the soul toward the good is, in one of its aspects, conscience, which, Philo tells us, "is born with our souls and dwells with them, and which always uses a nature that hates evil and loves virtue."[8]

[1] See *Cong.* 166 and cf. *Phaedr.* 256 B f.; *Symp.* 212 A.

[2] See *De cherub.* 20 and cf. *Symp.* 187 D; also *Quod Deus sit* 138; *De plant.* 22, 39; *De eb.* 136; *Quis rer. div.* 100, 310; *Cong.* 64; *Fug. et Inv.* 195; *Somn.* 1:36; *Conf. ling.* 106; *Mig. Ab.* 13, 58; *De praem.* 26; *De ag.* 55; *De op. mund.* 70; *Frg.* in M. 652, 669.

[3] Bréhier, *Id. phil. et relig.*, p. 275.

[4] *Symp.* 210 f. So, too, the power of the mythical ἀνάμνησις in *Phaedrus* 249 C ff. causes divine madness in the soul and leads the philosopher to shun the pursuits of men and to follow the divine.

[5] *Phaedr.* 250 A.

[6] Cf. the πρῶτον φίλον in *Lysis* 219, 220; *Symp.* 205 D, 210, 211; *Phaedr.* 250 D ff.; *Phil.* 64 E.

[7] *Phaedr.* 249 D E, 253 A, 256 B. Cf. Philo *Fug. et Inv.* 168 f.; *Mut. nom.* 39, 136; *De post. C.* 156–58; *Mig. Ab.* 34 f.; *De sob.* 27; *De eb.* 147 f.; *Quod det. pot.* 95.

[8] *Decal.* 87. For μισοπονήρῳ .... χρώμενος .... φύσει cf. Plato *Rep.* 366 C, θείᾳ φύσει δυσχεραίνων τὸ ἀδικεῖν. For other statements of the popular idea of conscience in Philo see *Conf. ling.* 121; *Quod det. pot.* 146; *De post. C.* 59; *Quod Deus sit* 128; *De eb.* 125; *De virt.* 206; *Fug. et Inv.* 159; *Somn.* 1:91; *De Jos.* 48, 68, 215, 262; *Sp. leg.* 1:235, 237.

This is the popular Greek notion of conscience. The article by W. H. S. Jones in Hastings' *Encyclopedia of Religion and Ethics*, IV, 38 ff., is a complete account of the Greek notions of conscience. Mr. Jones has there shown that the Greek ethical thinkers did not regard the mere feeling of right and wrong as of any great value. They emphasized enlightenment, knowledge of the good, rather than a mere feeling about it. It is in harmony with this that Plato, while he praises αἰδώς, yet regards it as the virtue of the many, not of the enlightened few.[1] The Idea of Good as a clearly formulated conception of what is finally desirable plays the part of the regulative conscience for the guardians of the ideal state, and for the others in that state its functions are given not to mere feeling but to right opinion based on the precepts of the leaders.[2] It is this enlightenment or knowledge of the good that Philo thinks of when he describes the "convictor" that comes into the soul from without and identifies it with the Logos[3] or with the disposition that is filled with heavenly Love.[4] There is, as has been pointed out before in this essay,[5] an element of rationalism in Philo and it is in accordance with this that, stripping off all mystic and popular unscientific ideas, he tells us that the conscience is, strictly speaking, merely the reason or intelligence that is in us.[6]

The third way of achieving perfection is, according to Philo, by instruction. There are two senses of παιδεία which must be distinguished. In one sense it means intellectual discipline, in another, training of the will by moral precepts and by the control of a superior.[7] The word is used in both senses by Plato.[8] The sage who attains virtue by instruction may according to the first sense be compared to the philosopher of Plato who goes from the many particulars to the unity they manifest.[9] Abraham is the type. He goes from the contemplation of the world to the contemplation of God.[10] He is the lover of instruction[11] who advances

---

[1] *Laws* 698 B, 699 C; *Rep.* 465 B. See Jones, *loc. cit.*

[2] *Rep.* 534 C D, 519 C D. For popular virtue see *Rep.* 429 C, 500 D, 501 B; *Gorg.* 503 E, 504 D; *Phaedo* 82 A B; *Pol.* 309 C D; *Laws* 632 C. Cf. Shorey, *Idea of Good*, p. 226; *Unity*, p. 16.

[3] *Fug. et Inv.* 117; *Quod Deus sit* 182.   [5] See above, pp. 11 f.

[4] *Quod Deus sit* 138.   [6] *Quod det. pot.* 22 f.

[7] For παιδεία in this second sense see *Fug. et Inv.* 172; *De sob.* 38; *Cong.* 69 f.

[8] Intellectual, *Rep.* 376 E; *Symp.* 187 D; *Laws* 641 B. Moral, *Laws* 653 C, 656 C, 803 D, 832 C D.

[9] *Phaedr.* 249 B f.; *Symp.* 210 f.

[10] *Mut. nom.* 76.   [11] *Quis rer. div.* 180.

by σκέψις.[1] He comes to have firm faith in the existence of God and in His providence.[2]

This intellectual discipline must begin with the μέσαι τεχναί or ἐπιστῆμαι, the ordinary Greek education of Philo's day. Gymnastics, geometry, grammar, arithmetic, music, rhetoric, and astronomy are mentioned.[3] These subjects are a necessary preliminary to the study of philosophy,[4] but they are only preliminary.[5] They give the mental discipline required and the taste for intellectual activity,[6] but they are not an end in themselves. Philo reproaches those who spend their lives in such studies.[7] These subjects require a special natural endowment as a preliminary.[8] Our finite minds can never come to the end of any one of them.[9] They depend on the senses for their data,[10] and so are connected with opinion, not with knowledge.[11] They deal with the particular, not the generic, sciences[12] and are the pursuit of the immature.[13]

In contrast to μέση παιδεία is philosophy, which deals with the generic sciences,[14] with the mind alone apart from the senses,[15] but using the data given by the senses and by the lesser sciences.[16] Its subject matter is the whole universe, all visible and invisible existence. The division is the same as in Plato. The μέση παιδεία corresponds to διάνοια of the divided line of the *Republic*, philosophy to dialectic.[17]

παιδεία stands also for instruction in the sense of the practical moral maxims one learns from teachers and the guidance of a superior

[1] *De op. mund.* 70. Note reminiscences of *Phaedrus* 249 B f. in πτηνὸς ἀρθείς . . . . ἔρωτι σοφίας ποδηγετοῦντι. Note ζήτησις, σκέψις, ἀκρόασις in *Quis rer. div.* 253; μάθησις, *De eb.* 83. Cf. *Mig. Ab.* 39; *Conf. ling.* 97; *Sp. leg.* 1:49; *Somn.* 1:59 f.

[2] *De praem.* 41–43.

[3] *Sp. leg.* 2:230; *De ag.* 18; *De eb.* 49; *Somn.* 1:205; *Quaes. in Gen.* 3:21; 4:14, 37, 256; *Quaes. in Ex.* 2:103, 535; *Sp. leg.* 1:336; *Cong.* 74. In *Cong.* 11–18 there is a discussion of the place of each subject.

[4] *Cong.* 74–76, 154, 156; *De eb.* 51.

[5] *De cherub.* 7, 8, 10; *De ag.* 9; *Mut. nom.* 73.

[6] *Quis rer. div.* 274.

[7] *De eb.* 51 f.; *Cong.* 73, 74, 77, 78.

[8] *Quis rer. div.* 121. Cf. Plato *Rep.* 518 A B.

[9] *De eb.* 53.

[10] *De post. C.* 137; *Cong.* 20, 22 f., 155 f.

[11] *De gig.* 60–62.

[12] *De cherub.* 7–10.

[13] *De eb.* 49 f.; *Somn.* 1:240 f.

[14] *De cherub.* 7–10.

[15] *Cong.* 155 f.; *Quis rer. div.* 111.

[16] *Cong.* 144 f.; *Frg.* in M. 654; *Conf. ling.* 97.

[17] See *Rep.* 518 A–521 A, and Shorey, *Idea of Good*, pp. 234 f. The distinction between νοῦς and διάνοια in Plato and between philosophy and μέση παιδεία in Philo is methodological.

mind.¹ Punishment is a necessary element of παιδεία in this sense.²
It is the inculcation of ideals of life by nurses, tutors, parents, the written
and unwritten laws. These may be false and lead to sin.³

The moral struggle against the passions is, along with παιδεία,⁴
a necessary feature in the life of most men.⁵ The man engaged in this
struggle is not altogether wicked. He has a love and zeal for the good,
but he is not perfectly good.⁶ He moves now upward, now downward.⁷
At the first stage he must not face temptation but must flee.⁸ Later he
must do battle with it.⁹ He has to undergo hard toil,¹⁰ but finally he
will be rewarded with perfection. His struggles end in peace.¹¹ He is
still engaged in the contest from which great good comes.¹²

In his utterances on the topic of the man in progress, Philo has
undoubtedly drawn from Stoic sources.¹³ There are suggestions of the
doctrine in Plato's recognition of the value of moral struggle, but the
emphasis on this struggle is Stoic in feeling. As often, Philo has
expanded the doctrine of Plato by Stoic elements. These elements are
not, however, inconsistent with Platonism or with the main trend of
Philo's own thought.

¹ See above, p. 85, n. 7. Cf. *Mut. nom.* 135 where it is classed with νουθεσία and σωφρονισμός; also *De post. C.* 71; *Fug. et Inv.* 207; *Mut. nom.* 229 (cf. διδασκαλία in *Fug. et Inv.* 200 f.). In *Leg. all.* 2:89–92 παιδεία has as its content the doctrine of the changeableness of all except God and the consequent faith in God alone. In § 92 the struggle against pleasure is itself described as παιδεία.

² *De post. C.* 97; *Cong.* 94.

³ *De sac. A et C.* 15; *De virt.* 178; *Quis rer. div.* 295; *Sp. leg.* 4:68; cf. Plato *Rep.* 549 E f.; *Protag.* 325 B–326 E.

⁴ Instruction and effort go together (*De Ab.* 53).

⁵ See *De sac. A. et C.* 111; *De ag.* 104, 177, 180; *De virt.* 10; *Mut. nom.* 34, 49 f., 213; *Sp. leg.* 2:47; *Quis rer. div.* 108; *De praem.* 26. Cf. Plato *Tim.* 51 E. God alone can be called σοφός: *Mig. Ab.* 134; *Cong.* 114; cf. Plato *Phaedr.* 278 D.

⁶ *Somn.* 1:150–52; 2:234–36; *De plant.* 94 ff. Cf. the philosopher in Plato *Symp.* 204 A.

⁷ *Somn.* 1:115, 150–52.   ⁹ *Leg. all.* 2:91; *Mig. Ab.* 27–31.

⁸ *Mig. Ab.* 26, 209.   ¹⁰ See above, p. 83, with n. 8.

¹¹ See above, p. 72, and cf. *De praem.* 36–40; *Mig. Ab.* 27, 30, 166. For the whole idea here cf. Hesiod. *O.D.* 287 ff. quoted in Plato *Laws* 718 E. Cf. *Phaedr.* 256 B.

¹² See above, p. 83, n. 8.

¹³ See Bréhier, *Id. phil. et relig.*, p. 267, with notes.

CHAPTER VI

THE INFLUENCE OF PLATO ON THE PHRASEOLOGY OF PHILO

The previous chapters have illustrated the influence of Plato on certain of the leading ideas of Philo and on the phraseology in which those ideas found expression. But the influence of Plato does not stop there. Philo seems to have brooded over Plato until the Platonic phraseology became a part of his own mind and his thoughts naturally, and at all times tended to be expressed in similar fashion. It is impossible within the limits of a single chapter even to approach completeness in such a subject. The most that will be attempted is to illustrate how, apart from explicit quotations,[1] striking passages of Plato are not only treated in detail but supply catch-words that recur again and again throughout Philo's works.[2]

1. THE FIGURE OF THE CHARIOT OF THE SOUL

The figure of the chariot of the soul, *Phaedrus* 246 A, 253 C–256 D, has penetrated into the very warp and woof of Philo's thought. The most detailed rendering of the Platonic passage is in *De ag.* 67–93. There are interesting variations from the Platonic myth. The team is made up of two horses, one male and one female, each of them bad, and the victory or defeat of reason is represented as due to the character of the reason that attempts to drive. The LXX word ἀναβάτης is taken to represent the reason that "mounts with folly," ἡνίοχος, that which "mounts with wisdom." When reason inclined to folly mounts, it is destroyed and the team then destroys both the chariot and itself. This destruction is a good, however, since it is a purification. When folly falls, wisdom arises.

After this preliminary exposition, the myth of Plato is used to explain three texts. The first is Deut. 20:1, "If thou goest forth to war against thy foes and seest a horse and rider (ἀναβάτης), be not afraid. The

---

[1] *Phaedr.* 247 A is quoted explicitly in *Quod omnis prob. lib.* 13; *Theaet.* 176 A B in *Fug. et Inv.* 63; *Theaet.* 191 C in *Quis rer. div.* 181; *Theaet.* 176 C in *Fug. et Inv.* 82; *Rep.* 473 D in *V.M.* 2:2. The *Symposium* is named and criticised in *De vit. cont.* 57–63.

[2] Siegfried, *Philo v. Alex.*, pp. 31–141, gives a study of Philo's style in relation to Greek literature. Pp. 32-37 contain a list of Platonic words. The citations from the *Timaeus* have been collected by Bréhier, *Id. phil. et relig.*, p. 78. See further, Conybeare, *De vit. cont.*, Index, p. 402, "Plato Imitated by Philo."

Lord thy God is with thee." This text, Philo says, means that God's power is our shield and champion against the passions and the reason that is inclined to folly.[1] The second is Ex. 15:1 and 21, the refrain of the Song of Moses and Miriam, "The Lord hath triumphed gloriously; the horse and his rider (ἀναβάτης) hath He cast into the sea." The downfall of the passions and of the reason inclined to folly is, Philo says, the greatest of victories. The third is Deut. 17:15 f., "Thou mayest not set a stranger over thee which is not thy brother, for he, that is the king, shall not multiply horses nor cause the people to return into Egypt." The literal explanation of this is rejected. It means that the reason inclined to folly and the pampering of the passions must not be allowed to rule. If it does get control, it is lost in the body, typified here by Egypt, the land of horses.

There are many reminiscences of the phraseology of the *Phaedrus* passage in this exposition. ὑψαύχην, *Phaedrus* 253 D, used by Plato in the description of the good horse, suggests Philo's characterization of the male, γαυριῶν ἄφετος εἶναι βούλεται καὶ ἐλεύθερος καὶ ἔστιν ὑψαύχην (§ 73). Note also τὸ . . . . ὑπέραυχον . . . . παθῶν τε καὶ κακιῶν . . . . στῖφος (§ 83). Another word in the *Phaedrus*, σκιρτῶν, 254 A, suggests σκιρτητικόν, in § 83 of the passage in Philo. ἐν νενικήκασιν, οὗ μεῖζον ἀγαθὸν οὔτε σωφροσύνη κ. τ. λ. of *Phaedrus* 256 B, suggests ἀμείνονα γὰρ καὶ τελειοτέραν οὐκ ἄν τις εὕροι σκοπῶν νίκην, Philo, § 83.

One of these interpretations plays a large part in Philo's allegorical exposition throughout. Horses are the passions; Egypt as the land of horses is the body, the seat of the passions; Pharaoh, the king of Egypt, is the mind that is inclined to folly.[2] In the passage before us, ἱπποτροφία, in sections 84 ff., carries on the figure and the myth is further suggested by νοῦν ἔποχον . . . . ἄπειρον ἱππικῆς ἐπιστήμης (§ 92), and τέχνην τὴν ἡνιοχικὴν (§ 93).

A curious instance of the way in which a phrase from the Platonic context may serve as a transition in Philo is seen in *De ag.* 94 f., the passage immediately following the one we have been considering. The suggestion comes from *Phaedrus* 254 B, ἰδόντος δὲ τοῦ ἡνιόχου ἡ μνήμη πρὸς τὴν τοῦ κάλλους φύσιν ἠνέχθη, καὶ πάλιν εἶδεν αὐτὴν μετὰ σωφροσύνης ἐν ἁγνῷ βάθρῳ βεβῶσαν· ἰδοῦσα δὲ ἔδεισέ τε καὶ σεφθεῖσα ἀνέπεσεν ὑπτία. Cf. 254 E, ὁ δ' ἡνίοχος . . . . ὥσπερ ἀπὸ ὕσπληγος ἀναπεσών. These phrases in the context of the Platonic figure he is developing suggest

[1] This text is similarly interpreted in *Mig. Ab.* 62.

[2] Egypt, the land of the senses: *Leg. all.* 2:77, 3:37 f., 212 f.; *De sac. A et C.* 51, 62; *Quod det. pot.* 38; *De post. C.* 62 f.; 96. Pharaoh as the mind inclined to folly: *De sac. A. et C.* 9 f.; 69 f.; *Quod det. pot.* 95, 161 f.

to Philo the passage in Gen. 49:17 f., γενέσθω Δᾶν ὄφις ἐφ' ὁδοῦ, ἐγκαθήμενος ἐπὶ τρίβου, δάκνων πτέρναν ἵππου, καὶ πεσεῖται ὁ ἱππεὺς εἰς τὰ ὀπίσω, τὴν σωτηρίαν περιμένων κυρίου.[1] Dan, Philo says, means κρίσις. κρίσις is a serpent, not that which tempted Eve and which is called pleasure, but that which Moses made for the healing of the nation, which symbolizes καρτερία, the disposition opposed to pleasure. It therefore serves the same purpose here as memory does in the Platonic passage. The horse whose heel is bitten is described in § 109 as "the symbol of passion and wickedness." κρίσις or καρτερία bites, since "temperance practises the purgation and destruction of these things." In § 110 the phrase ὁ ἱππεὺς πεσεῖται is explained. "The riddle," Philo says, "is as follows. He (Moses) regards it as good and as worth striving for that our intelligence should be mounted on none of the things that rise from passion or vice, and, when it has been compelled to mount any one of them, that it should be eager to change and to fall off. For such falls bring the most glorious victories." Cf. *Phaedrus* 256 B, τῶν τριῶν παλαισμάτων τῶν ὡς ἀληθῶς Ὀλυμπιακῶν ἓν νενικήκασιν οὗ μεῖζον ἀγαθὸν οὔτε σωφροσύνη ἀνθρωπίνη οὔτε θεία μανία δυνατὴ πορίσαι ἀνθρώπῳ.[2] The fall which is a victory[3] suggests the victory which is a defeat, the victory in a contest of evil (§ 111).[4] Philo urges that the prizes in such contests be eagerly given up (§ 112). The prizes of the truly sacred contests men are urged to bind on their own brows (§113). The truly sacred contests are not the public games.[5] These are to be despised by men of sense. (§§ 113–19). ὁ τοίνυν Ὀλυμπιακὸς ἀγὼν μόνος ἂν λέγοιτο ἐνδίκως ἱερός, οὐχ ὃν τιθέασιν οἱ τὴν Ἦλιν οἰκοῦντες, ἀλλ' ὁ περὶ κτήσεως τῶν θείων καὶ ὀλυμπίων ὡς ἀληθῶς ἀρετῶν. This whole passage has again been suggested by a phrase in the Platonic context.[6]

[1] *Leg. all.* 2:99–104 contains a similar exposition of this text and Ex. 15.1 with many reminiscences of the *Phaedrus* passages quoted above.

[2] Cf. *Laws* 840 B, πολὺ καλλίονος ἕνεκα νίκης, ἣν ἡμεῖς καλλίστην . . . . ᾄδοντες . . . . τῆς τῶν ἡδονῶν νίκης.

[3] Cf. *Somn.* 1:131, ἡττᾶσθαι δοκοῦσα νικηφορήσει.

[4] For contests in wickedness see *De Ab.* 40; *Sp. leg.* 1:330.

[5] For ἱερὸς ἀγών, cf. *De Ab.* 48; *De praem.* 52; *Mut. nom.* 81, 106. Cf. ἀθληταὶ τῷ ὄντι ἀρετῆς, *De praem.* 5.

[6] For another case where Philo has evidently worked with the text of Plato before him see Conybeare, *De vita contemplativa*, p. 276. In the description of the greedy banqueter (§ 53), Conybeare notices the occurrence of the words περιάγοντες τοὺς αὐχένας adapted from *Rep.* 515 C. It was, he thinks, the use of these words from a philosophic context that suggested the development of the figure of the greedy banqueter in regard to wisdom in *Somn.* 1:49 f. In working out this figure Philo "glances afresh at the *Republic* of Plato, borrowing from a contiguous passage thereof (514 B) the use of τὴν κεφαλήν instead of τοὺς αὐχένας after περιάγοντες."

The figure of the passions as horses is developed briefly in *Leg. all.* 1:72 f. and 3:118, 128. The phraseology suggests it in many other passages. Cf. τὸ τῆς ψυχῆς ὄχημα (*Leg. all.* 2:85); ἡνιόχου τρόπον ἐπιστομίζῃ (*Leg. all.* 3:134); τὸν λόγον ὡσανεί τινα ἡνίοχον εὐθύνοντα σκληραύχενα καὶ ἀφηνιαστὴν ἵππον (*Leg. all.* 3:136); ὥσπερ οὖν ἄρχοντος μὲν ἡνιόχου καὶ ταῖς ἡνίαις τὰ ζῷα ἄγοντος ᾗ βούλεται ἄγεται τὸ ἅρμα, ἀφηνιασάντων δὲ ἐκείνων καὶ κρατησάντων ὅ τε ἡνίοχος κατεσύρη πολλάκις τά τε ζῷα ἔστιν ὅτε τῇ ῥύμῃ τῆς φορᾶς εἰς βόθρον κατηνέχθη (*Leg. all.* 3:223); πῇ μὲν γὰρ ἐπανιέναι δεῖ καθάπερ ἡνίοχον τοῖς ὑπεζευγμένοις τὰς ἡνίας, πῇ δὲ ἀντισπᾶν καὶ ἀναχαιτίζειν, ὁπότε πλείων ἡ πρὸς τὰ ἐκτὸς ῥύμη καὶ φορὰ σὺν ἀφηνιασμῷ γίνοιτο (*De sac. A. et C.* 49).[1]

The figure is often combined with that of the pilot, used in *Phaedrus* 247 C in the midst of the myth of the chariot of the soul. So in *De sac. A. et C.* 45, Philo speaks of τῶν κατὰ ψυχὴν ἀλόγων δυνάμεων ἡνίοχός τε καὶ κυβερνήτης. Compare *Leg. all.* 2:104, 3:118, 224; *De sac. A. et C.* 105; *Quod det. pot.* 53, 141; *Mig. Ab.* 67; *Conf. ling.* 115.

The figure of νοῦς as the pilot of the soul is used alone in *Sp. leg.* 4:95 and is suggested in *Somn.* 2:147. It is combined with suggestions from the figure of the ship of state (*Rep.* 487 E–489 C) in *Quod Deus sit* 129: ἔχουσα γὰρ ἡ ψυχὴ τὸν ὑγιαίνοντα καὶ ζωτικὸν καὶ ὀρθὸν ἐν ἑαυτῷ λόγον τῷ μὲν οὐ χρῆται ὡς κυβερνήτῃ πρὸς τὴν τῶν καλῶν σωτηρίαν, ἐκδοῦσα δ' αὐτὴν τοῖς ναυτιλίας ἀπείροις, κ. ἵτ. λ. Cf. *Conf. ling.* 22. There are further suggestions from this passage of the *Republic* in *Fug. et Inv.* 27, *Sp. leg.* 4:153–56, *Frg. from J. of A.* 775 E (M., p. 657).

The figure of νοῦς as the pilot of the soul suggests that of the soul itself as a ship. This last is interjected into the midst of Philo's development of the figure of the chariot of the soul in *De ag.* 89.

He that has a multitude of horses in his stables must necessarily tread the way to Egypt. For when along the sides of the soul, which is like a ship, whose sides are reason and sensation, which rocks and tips under the violence of the passions and sins that blow upon it, there comes a great wave, then, as is to be expected, the reason is swamped and sunk. And the deep into which it is overwhelmed and sunk is the body which is likened to Egypt.

[1] Compare the use of ἀπαυχενίζω in *Quis rer. div.* 245; *De ag.* 34; *Sp. leg.* 1:304; ὑψαυχενοῦν, *Leg. all.* 3:18; ὑπέραυχον, *De ag.* 62; σκληραύχενα, *Somn.* 2:80; ἀφηνιάζω, *Cong.* 118, 158; *V.M.* 1:26; *De eb.* 15, 111; *De sac. A. et C.* 45; *De virt.* 13; *Sp. leg.* 4:79; ἐγχαλινόω, *Leg. all.* 3:155; *Quod det. pot.* 53; ἀχαλίνωτον, *Conf. ling.* 165; *V.M.* 1:25; *Sp. leg.* 4:79; σκιρτάω, *Quis rer. div.* 245; *De ag.* 34; *Sp. leg.* 1:304; χρεματίζω or φρυάττομαι, *Fug. et Inv.* 107; *De cherub.* 66; *Quod Deus sit* 168; cf. *Leg. all.* 3:193.

This passage has suggestions also from the figure of the storm in *Rep.* 496 D and from the figure of the body as a river into which the soul is sunk in *Timaeus* 43 A.[1] Cf. with the latter κατακλυσθεῖσαν ὑπὸ τοῦ τοιούτου ψόγου, *Rep.* 492 C. The figure blends with the common metaphorical use of σαλεύω and σάλος[2] in many passages, notably *Leg. all.* 2:90; *Decal.* 67; *De cherub.* 13; *Frg. from Eus.* 8:13 (M., p. 635).

2. THE FIGURE OF THE CONTEST

The figure of the contest is common in Philo[3] and there are reminiscences of other Platonic passages than the reference to the Olympic games in *Phaedrus* 256 B.[4] In *Rep.* 504 A the struggle with difficult μαθήματα is compared to the struggle in the athletic contests. The guardians are said to be tested εἴτε καὶ ἀποδειλιάσει ὥσπερ οἱ ἐν τοῖς ἄθλοις ἀποδειλιῶντες. There is a reminiscence of this passage in *De praem.* 29. The λογισμός, when it thinks that its judgments are joined to the intelligible, the self-consistent and abiding, is convicted of pining for many things. For when it approaches the vast number of particulars it loses its strength and grows weak and faint καθάπερ ἀθλητὴς ὑπὸ ῥώμης δυνατωτέρας ἐκτραχηλιζόμενος. The metaphor is shifted. The defeat of the reason is due to superior force in Philo. In Plato the defeat is due to cowardice. The figure of the contest is, however, similarly applied. καθάπερ ἐν ἄθλοις is used in the same way in *Sp. leg.* 1:38, where the contest is the effort to see the truth.

It is characteristic of Philo's elaborately metaphorical style that he carries this figure into details. The preliminary exercises and contests in which the athlete must engage;[5] the decisions by which those incapable of competing are rejected;[6] the struggle itself;[7] pauses in the

[1] Many passages in Philo carry out this figure of the river or torrent of the senses. Cf. *De gig.* 13; *Fug. et Inv.* 49; *Somn.* 2:109; *Sp. leg.* 2:147; *Quod det. pot.* 100, 170; and see above, pp. 69, 70.

[2] Noticed by Liddell and Scott, *s.v.*, σαλεύω, II.

[3] Cf. supra, p. 83, n. 8; p. 87.

[4] Cf. also in Plato *Rep.* 403 E; *Laws* 830 A, 840 B, *et al.*

[5] Isaac, for example, is said to be γυμναζόμενος ἀθλητοῦ τρόπον by his trials, *De Jos.* 223. Cf. *V.M.* 1:106; *Somn.* 1:131; *Mut. nom.* 81.

[6] *Mut. nom.* 106; cf. *Fug. et Inv.* 40.

[7] Against ignorance, *Sp. leg.* 1:38; against pleasure, cf. above, p. 90; also *De ag.* 180; *Leg. all.* 3:18; *Quod omnis prob. lib.* 26 f., 110–13; against grief, *De Ab.* 256; against ill-fortune, *Somn.* 2:145 f.; *Quod Deus sit* 13. For the competition in wickedness, see above, p. 90, n. 4.

contests;[1] victory and defeat;[2] the rewards of victory;[3] all these furnish metaphors in Philo. It is the figure used by Plato elaborated and carried into details.[4]

3. FIGURE OF THE HEALTH AND DISEASE OF THE SOUL

The figure of the health and disease of the soul which is common in Plato is also very frequent in Philo. The passions are diseases of the soul. Cf. *Timaeus* 86 B with *De virt.* 162; *Quod Deus sit* 67; *Sp. leg.* 1:237, 239, 253, 281; 4:83; *Mig. Ab.* 155, 219; *Cong.* 93; *De sob.* 45; *Quis rer. div.* 297; *Somn.* 1:69; 2:299; *De vit. cont.* 2; *Leg. all.* 3:211. Virtue is health. *Rep.* 444 D E, 591 B C; *Gorg.* 512 A, 479 B; *Crito* 47 D E. In Philo *De eb.* 140 f.; *Conf. ling.* 22, 25; *Mig. Ab.* 119; *Quis rer. div.* 299; *De Ab.* 26, 275; *V.M.* 2:185; *Sp. leg.* 4:182, 237. Cf. εὐταξία, the mother of εὐεξία, in *Frg.* (M., p. 674), and for εὐταξία, cf. *Gorg.* 504 B, for εὐεξία, *Timaeus* 86 E, διὰ δὲ πονηρὰν ἕξιν. The passage on memory, recollection, and forgetfulness as respectively health, recovery, and disease (*Cong.* 39–42) is suggested by *Timaeus* 87 A where λήθη is listed among the diseases of the soul. The disease of cowardice mentioned in the same passage is dealt with in *De virt.* 26.

The notion of incurable disease of the soul occurs in several Platonic passages and is so common in Philo as to develop into a catch-word applied in contexts foreign to Plato. The passage in *Laws* 862 D E has directly influenced one passage in Philo. The sentence in Plato is ὃν δ' ἂν ἀνιάτως εἰς ταῦτα ἔχοντα . . . . θάνατον ἀνάγκη νέμειν. In *De eb.* 28, Philo has οἱ ὑπαίτιοι καὶ ἐπίληπτοι λογισμοί, οὕς, ὁπότε ἀνιάτως ἔχοιεν, ἀποκόπτειν καὶ διαφθείρειν ἀναγκαῖον. Cf. *De ag.* 40, κολάσει χρώμενοι . . . . ἀφορήτῳ δὲ κατὰ τῶν ἀνίατα (νεωτεριζόντων). Other instances of the occurrence of the idea of incurable disease of the soul in Plato are *Rep.* 615 E; *Phaedo* 113 E; *Gorg.* 480 B, 525 C. Compare in Philo *De cherub.* 2, 10, 42; *De post. C.* 11, 74; *Quod det. pot.* 178; *Somn.* 2:196; *De Ab.* 115; *De eb.* 18, 140, 223; *Mig. Ab.* 210; *De gig.* 35; *Mut. nom.* 144; *Sp. Leg.* 2:17; 3:11; *De virt.* 4; *Frg.* (M., p. 655). The figure

---

[1] *Leg. all.* 3:14; *De praem.* 157; *Sp. leg.* 4:214.

[2] *De praem.* 5 f., 52; *De plant.* 145; *De Ab.* 35.

[3] *Leg. all.* 1:81, 2:108, 3:48, 74; *De Ab.* 35, 129; *Quis rer. div.* 47; *Mig. Ab.* 26–30, 133 f., 199 f.; *Mut. nom.* 48; *De eb.* 34 f.; *Cong.* 159, 162, 165; *Fug. et Inv.* 187. For the figure of the δευτερεῖα in Plato cf. *Phil.* 22 E, 33 C, 61 A.

[4] For a somewhat similar elaboration of a Platonic figure see the discussion of *Phaedr.* 259 C in connection with its Philonic echoes in Conybeare, p. 277, and compare the use of ἀέρι τρέφεσθαι in the *Testimonia* cited in Conybeare, *op. cit.*, p. 73, on l. 49.

develops so far toward being a mere catchword that it is used of famine (ἔνδεια) in *De Jos.* 191. Cf. *De Jos.* 110, 113, 160 f. The flood is called a disease of the κόσμος in *De Ab.* 46.

The metaphor of the healing of such diseases of the soul as can be cured is one that Philo uses with frequent reminiscences of Plato. Punishment, instruction, dialectic, ὀρθὸς λόγος, association with the good, conscience, and the direct influence of the divine are the remedial agents. The notion of the remedial office of punishment is common in Plato. See *Gorgias* 478 B-479 C; *Laws* 862 D E, 854 D, 934 A, 944 D; *Rep.* 616 A.[1] The influence of Platonic ideas is seen in *Quod det. pot.* 144, διό μοι δοκοῦσιν οἱ μὴ τελείως δυσκάθαρτοι εὔξασθαι ἂν κολασθῆναι μᾶλλον ἢ ἀφεθῆναι . . . . ἡ δὲ κόλασις ἐπανορθώσεται. Cf. *Somn.* 2:294 f.; *Cong.* 157-62, 167, 172, 175, 177-80. The passage in *Protag.* 325 C D has influenced the phraseology of Philo in several passages. It reads: ἐπειδὰν θᾶττον συνιῇ τις τὰ λεγόμενα, καὶ τροφὸς καὶ μήτηρ καὶ παιδαγωγὸς καὶ αὐτὸς ὁ πατὴρ περὶ τούτου διαμάχονται, ὅπως ὡς βέλτιστος ἔσται παῖς, ... καὶ ἐὰν μὲν ἑκὼν πείθηται· εἰ δὲ μή, ὥσπερ ξύλον διαστρεφόμενον καὶ καμπτόμενον εὐθύνουσιν ἀπειλαῖς καὶ πληγαῖς. Next follow διδάσκαλοι, and then (326 C) ἡ πόλις αὖ τούς τε νόμους ἀναγκάζει μανθάνειν καὶ κατὰ τούτους ζῆν κατὰ παράδειγμα. Cf. *Mig. Ab.* 116, σωφρονιστῶν ὡς ἔοικε τοῦτό ἐστι τὸ ἔθος, παιδαγωγῶν, διδασκάλων, γονέων, πρεσβυτέρων, ἀρχόντων, νόμων· ὀνειδίζοντες γάρ, ἔστι δ' ὅπου καὶ κολάζοντες ἔκαστοι τούτων ἀμείνους τὰς ψυχὰς ἀπεργάζονται τῶν παιδευομένων. Also *De sob.* 23, τὰς τῶν γονέων καὶ τρεφόντων ὠφελιμωτάτας μὲν ἀτερπεστάτας δὲ ὑφηγήσεις. In *De eb.* 141 παιδεία heals the disease of the soul. ὑγιεινὸν μὲν καὶ σωτήριον χρῆμα παιδεία, νόσου δὲ καὶ φθορᾶς αἴτιον ἀπαιδευσία. So in *Rep.* 430 A B ὅτε ἐξελεγόμεθα τοὺς στρατιώτας καὶ ἐπαιδεύομεν μουσικῇ καὶ γυμναστικῇ μηδὲν οἶον ἄλλο μηχανᾶσθαι ἢ ὅπως . . . . δέξοιντο ὥσπερ βαφήν . . . . καὶ μὴ αὐτῶν ἐκπλῦναι τὴν βαφὴν τὰ ῥύμματα ταῦτα, ... ἡδονή, ... λύπη τε καὶ φόβος καὶ ἐπιθυμία, ... τὴν δὴ τοιαύτην δύναμιν καὶ σωτηρίαν κ. τ. λ. Philosophy is the cure in *Quis rer. div.* 297, ταύτην τὴν ἐπίνοσον γενεὰν . . . ·. οἷα ὑπὸ ἰατρικῆς φιλοσοφίας νοσηλευθῆναι χρή. Cf. *Decal.* 150, λόγος ὁ κατὰ φιλοσοφίαν ἰατροῦ δίκην ἀγαθοῦ. The figure affects the language in *Cong.* 53 where λογοπῶλαι and λογοθῆραι are compared to those who seek to cure by λογιατρεία.

A metaphor closely allied to this comes from *Phaedo* 82 E-83 A— γιγνώσκουσιν οἱ φιλομαθεῖς ὅτι οὕτω παραλαβοῦσα ἡ φιλοσοφία ἔχουσαν

---

[1] On Plato's theory of punishment see Adam, *The Republic of Plato*, I, 117, note to 380 B.

αὐτῶν τὴν ψυχὴν . . . . ἐνδεικνυμένη ὅτι ἀπάτης μὲν μεστὴ ἡ διὰ τῶν ὀμμάτων σκέψις, ... καὶ τῶν ἄλλων αἰσθήσεων, πείθουσα δὲ ἐκ τούτων μὲν ἀναχωρεῖν. Philonic reminiscences of this passage appear in Cong. 18, διαλεκτικὴ . . . . μεγάλην νόσον ψυχῆς ἀπάτην ἀκέσεται, and V.M. 2:66, φύσεως εὐμοιρίᾳ χρησάμενος, ἥν, ὥσπερ ἀγαθὴν ἄρουραν, φιλοσοφία παραλαβοῦσα κ. τ. λ.

As sick men go to physicians, so, Philo tells us in Quod omnis prob. lib. 12, we should become σοφῶν ἀνδρῶν ὁμιληταί,[1] for by their help it is possible to rid one's self of ἀμαθία and to take the peculiar possession of man, knowledge. In the description of εὐλάβεια in Laws 854 B C, one prescription is ἴθι ἐπὶ τὰς τῶν λεγομένων ἀνδρῶν ὑμῖν ἀγαθῶν συνουσίας . . . . ἐὰν μέν σοι δρῶντι ταῦτα λωφᾷ τι τὸ νόσημα. So also with τὰς δὲ τῶν κακῶν συνουσίας φεῦγε ἀμεταστρεπτί compare οὗτοι τὸ μὲν πρῶτον κωμῃδὸν οἰκοῦσι τὰς πόλεις ἐκτρεπόμενοι διὰ τὰς τῶν πολιτευομένων χειροήθεις ἀνομίας, εἰδότες ἐκ τῶν συνόντων ὡς ἀπ' ἀέρος φθοροποιοῦ νόσον ἐγγινομένην προσβολὴν ψυχαῖς ἀνίατον (Quod omnis prob. lib. 76).

ὀρθὸς λόγος is the physician of sin in Sp. leg. 2:31. Cf. τὴν τοιαύτην δύναμιν καὶ σωτηρίαν διὰ παντὸς δόξης ὀρθῆς, in Rep. 430 B. Compare conscience as the physician in Sp. leg. 1:237, Quod Deus sit 182, and Logoi as healing the soul in Somn. 1:69. For God as the healer see De virt. 26. Cowardice is said to grow with our growth, εἰ μὴ τύχοι θεὸς ἰώμενος, πάντα γὰρ θεῷ δυνατά. Compare Rep. 493 A, θεοῦ μοῖραν αὐτὸ σῶσαι λέγων οὐ κακῶς ἐρεῖς. Compare Meno 99 E.

4. FIGURE OF THE BODYGUARDS

In Rep. 566 B, in his account of the genesis of the tyrannical state, Plato tells of the notorious request of the tyrant, the request that the people grant him φύλακάς τινας τοῦ σώματος. In 567 D he tells us ὅσῳ ἂν μᾶλλον τοῖς πολίταις ἀπεχθάνηται . . . . τοσούτῳ πλειόνων καὶ πιστοτέρων δορυφόρων δεήσεται. In 573 A, in depicting the genesis of the tyrannical man, Plato makes use of the idea of the bodyguard as a metaphor. The tyrant desire ὅταν δὴ περὶ αὐτὸν βομβοῦσαι αἱ ἄλλαι ἐπιθυμίαι, ... πόθου κέντρον ἐμποιήσωσι τῷ κηφῆνι, τότε δὴ δορυφορεῖται ὑπὸ μανίας καὶ οἴστρᾳ. This is one of the common metaphors in Philo. He develops the Platonic figure and applies it to the senses. Somn. 1:27 is an instance of Philo's use of this metaphor. The senses, ἄγγελοι διανοίας εἰσὶ διαγγέλουσαι χρώματα, σχήματα, φωνάς, ἀτμῶν καὶ χυλῶν ἰδιότητας . . . . καὶ . . . . δορυφόροι ψυχῆς εἰσιν, ὅσα ἂν ἴδωσιν ἢ ἀκούσωσι δηλοῦσαι κἂν εἴ τι

[1] Cf. περὶ τὴν ψυχὴν αὖ ἰατρικὸς, Protag. 313 E.

βλαβερὸν ἔξωθεν ἐπίοι προορώμεναί τε καὶ φυλαττόμεναι.¹ Compare *Sp. leg.* 3:111; 4:92, 123; *Somn.* 1:32; *De op. mund.* 139; *Leg. all.* 3:115; *Quod det. pot.* 33, 85. There are other applications of the figure. Goods are divided into external goods, goods of the body, and goods of the soul. The external goods are the bodyguard of the goods of the body and these in turn are the bodyguard of the goods of the soul. See *De eb.* 201; *De sob.* 62; *Conf. ling.* 17–20; *Quis rer. div.* 285; *De virt.* 8. The powers of God are His bodyguards (*Quod Deus sit* 109; *De Ab.* 122; *Sp. leg.* 1:45). So the planets are the bodyguard of the sun (*Quis rer. div.* 223). νοῦς has as its attendants οἱ κατὰ μέρος δορυφοροῦντες λογισμοί (*Mut. nom.* 21). Speech is a δορυφόρος of a man, guarding him against his foes (*Somn.* 1:103). The idea in the last passage is suggested by the speech of Callicles in *Gorgias* 486 B C. Cf. with the passage in the *Gorgias*, τούτῳ δὲ προαγωνιστῇ χρώμενος δυνήσεται τὰς ἀπὸ τῶν ἐχθρῶν ἐπιφερομένας ἀπωθεῖσθαι ζημίας,— δεύτερον δὲ καὶ αἰσχύνης καὶ ὀνειδῶν ἀναγκαιότατον περίβλημα—δεινὸς γὰρ συγκρύψαι καὶ συσκιάσαι τὰς ἁμαρτίας τῶν ἀνθρώπων λόγος (*Somn.* 1:103 f.).

5. THE FIGURE OF THE PREGNANT MIND

The familiar passage on Socrates as the midwife, *Theaet.* 150 B–151 D, has influenced Philo's language in many passages. A striking instance is in *Quis rer. div.* 247: μέχρις ἂν ὁ μαιευτικὸς ὁμοῦ καὶ δικαστικὸς ἀνὴρ συγκαθίσας θεάσηται τὰ τῆς ἑκάστου γεννήματα ψυχῆς καὶ τὰ μὲν οὐκ ἄξια τροφῆς ἀπορρίψῃ, τὰ δ' ἐπιτήδεια διασώσῃ καὶ προνοίας τῆς ἁρμοττούσης ἀξιώσῃ. Compare *Theaet.* 150 B C, μέγιστον δὲ τοῦτ' ἔνι τῇ ἡμετέρᾳ τέχνῃ, βασανίζειν δυνατὸν εἶναι παντὶ τρόπῳ πότερον εἴδωλον καὶ ψεῦδος ἀποτίκτει τοῦ νέου ἡ διάνοια ἢ γόνιμόν τε καὶ ἀληθές.² In Philo's usual manner, the figure is extended and applied to the moral rather than the intellectual sphere. So in *De sac. A. et C.* 102 f., ὥσπερ γὰρ ταῖς γυναιξὶ πρὸς ζῴων γένεσιν οἰκειότατον μέρος ἡ φύσις ἔδωκε μήτραν, οὕτως πρὸς γένεσιν πραγμάτων ὥρισεν ἐν ψυχῇ δύναμιν, δι' ἧς κυοφορεῖ καὶ ὠδίνει καὶ ἀποτίκτει πολλὰ διάνοια. τῶν δὲ ἀποκυουμένων ἐννοημάτων τὰ μὲν ἄρρενα, τὰ δὲ θήλεα, καθάπερ ἐπὶ ζῴων εἶναι συμβέβηκε. θῆλυ μὲν οὖν ἔγγονον ψυχῆς ἐστι κακία καὶ πάθος, οἷς καθ' ἕκαστον τῶν ἐπιτηδευμάτων ἐκθηλυνόμεθα, ἄρρεν δὲ εὐπάθεια καὶ ἀρετή, ὑφ' ὧν ἐγειρόμεθα καὶ ῥωννύμεθα.

Philo bases his interpretation of Gen. 6:4, in *Quod Deus sit* 1–9, on this same figure. The text reads: καὶ μετ' ἐκεῖνο ὡς ἂν εἰσεπορεύοντο οἱ

---

[1] For ἄγγελοι cf. *Rep.* 523 C–524 B. Note especially ἐσήμηνεν (523 D); δηλοῦσιν (523 E); παραγγέλλει (524 A); σημαίνει (524 A); ἑρμηνεῖαι (524 B); τῶν εἰσαγγελλομένων (524 B); σαφηνείαν (524 C).

[2] Cf. also *Theaet.* 151 C, 157 D, 160 E, 210 C.

ἄγγελοι τοῦ θεοῦ πρὸς τὰς θυγατέρας τῶν ἀνθρώπων, καὶ ἐγέννων αὐτοῖς. This means, he says, that the comrades of darkness, those that bear false messages, wax strong and go in unto the weak and effeminate passions and beget offspring for themselves, not for God. The true offspring of God are the perfect virtues, but the kindred of the wicked are the incongruous vices. Abraham is the type of the man who does not beget offspring for himself. He offered up to God his son Isaac, who represents the wisdom that comes spontaneously in the soul. One of those who were like him was Hannah, "who became pregnant, receiving the divine seed, and experienced the birth-pangs that brought fulness of accomplishment, bringing forth the character that is appointed in the company of God." In this development of the figure, God impregnates the soul with virtue.

In sections 10–15 of the same treatise, Philo develops the figure still further, making use of another passage of the *Theaetetus*. The section is an explanation of I Kings 2:5, στεῖρα ἔτεκεν ἑπτά, ἡ δὲ πολλὴ ἐν τέκνοις ἠσθένησε. Hannah, who had but one child, is said to have borne seven, since seven and one are the same in their qualities. It was natural that she who was στεῖραν, οὐ τὴν ἄγονον, ἀλλὰ τὴν στερρὰν καὶ ἔτι σφριγῶσαν (§ 13), who struggled to the end in the contests that are through endurance and courage and patience for the possession of the best, should bring forth the monad equal in honor with seven. The explanation of the second part of the text, ἡ δὲ πολλὴ ἐν τέκνοις ἠσθένησε, is connected with *Theaet*. 156 A where Socrates explains the origin of sense perception. The active and the passive come together, he says, ἐκ δὲ τῆς τούτων ὁμιλίας τε καὶ τρίψεως πρὸς ἄλληλα γίγνεται ἔκγονα πλήθει μὲν ἄπειρα, δίδυμα δέ, τὸ μὲν αἰσθητόν, τὸ δὲ αἴσθησις, ἀεὶ συνεκπίπτουσα καὶ γεννωμένη μετὰ τοῦ αἰσθητοῦ. αἱ μὲν οὖν αἰσθήσεις τὰ τοιάδε ἡμῖν ἔχουσιν ὀνόματα, ὄψεις τε καὶ ἀκοαὶ καὶ ὀσφρήσεις καὶ ψύξεις τε καὶ καύσεις καὶ ἡδοναί γε δὴ καὶ λῦπαι καὶ ἐπιθυμίαι καὶ φόβοι κεκλημέναι καὶ ἄλλαι, ἀπέραντοι μὲν αἱ ἀνώνυμοι, παμπληθεῖς δὲ αἱ ὠνομασμέναι. Philo says (§ 14) that when the soul, which is one, separates itself from the One, it has many birth-pangs—μυρία κατὰ τὸ εἰκὸς γίνεται (compare Plato's γίγνεται ἔκγονα πλήθει μὲν ἄπειρα) κἄπειτα πλήθει τέκνων ἐξηρτημένων βαρυνομένη καὶ πιεζομένη . . . . ἐξασθενεῖ. His hostility to the senses leads him to add a metaphor from *Theaet*. 150 C hardly consistent here. ἔστι δὲ ἠλιτόμηνα καὶ ἀμβλωθρίδια τὰ πλεῖστα αὐτῶν. The rest of the section (15 ff.) shows a close parallel with *Theaet*. 156 A: τίκτει μὲν γὰρ τὰς πρὸς σχήματα καὶ χρώματα δι' ὀφθαλμῶν ἐπιθυμίας, τίκτει δὲ τὰς πρὸς φωνὰς δι' ὤτων, ἐγκύμων δ' ἐστὶ καὶ τῶν γαστρὸς καὶ τῶν ὑπ' αὐτήν. The same metaphor is applied to sensation in *Leg. all.* 3:216, where αἴσθησις is the mother of τὸ αἰσθάνεσθαι.

The conception of God as the father of the child of the mind is developed in a number of passages besides those already quoted. A noteworthy instance is *De cherub.* 42 f. What is here said, Philo tells us, is a divine mystery and is to be revealed only to the initiated. Sarah, Rebekah, Leah, and Moses' wife Sepphora were not women but virtues. They became pregnant from God (43). God is then σοφίας ἀνὴρ σπέρμα τῷ θνητῷ γένει καταβαλλόμενος εὐδαιμονίας εἰς ἀγαθὴν καὶ παρθένον γῆν (49). The same figure is developed in *Leg. all.* 3:216–19, where God is the father by virtue of χαρά, or τὸ εὐδαιμονεῖν. In *Leg. all.* 3:180 f. God is the father of the virtues conceived in the soul.[1]

6. FIGURES REPRESENTING THE SENSES AND THE PASSIONS

Philo's use of the figure of the horses to represent the passions has already been dealt with (pp. 88 ff.). At times the passions are described under the figure suggested by θρέμμα ἄγριον in *Timaeus* 70 E, θηρίον in *Phaedrus* 230 A and τὸ παντοδαπὸν θηρίον in *Rep.* 588 C ff.[2] So in *Leg. all.* 2:9 and 3:113, τὰ πάθη τῆς ψυχῆς are called θηρία. In *Mig. Ab.* 212, Haran, θρεμμάτων μὲν ἀνάπλεως, οἰκήτορσι δὲ κεχρημένη κτηνοτρόφοις, is the land of the senses. Cf. *Somn.* 2:267; *De ag.* 39; *De plant.* 43. In contrast to the senses, the mind or reason is ὁ πρὸς ἀλήθειαν ἄνθρωπος in *Fug. et Inv.* 71 f.; cf. *Rep.* 589 A B.

Sense is frequently spoken of as the woman in the soul. The figure comes from *Timaeus* 42 A: διπλῆς δὲ οὔσης τῆς ἀνθρωπίνης φύσεως, τὸ κρεῖττον τοιοῦτον εἴη γένος ὃ καὶ ἔπειτα κεκλήσοιτο ἀνήρ. On a basis of this passage Philo makes Eve the symbol of sense in *Leg. all.* 2:38. Compare πάντα δὲ κακίας καὶ παθῶν, ὧν γυναικώδεις αἱ βλάσται, *De gig.* 4; cf. 18. So in *Sp. leg.* 3:178, the male soul is said to devote itself to God alone, the female soul depends on becoming and the corruptible. In *De op. mund.* 165, νοῦς possesses the soul of the man, αἴσθησις that of the woman. Cf. *Sp. leg.* 1:201.

7. PHRASEOLOGY SUGGESTING THE PLATONIC IDEAS

Philo's doctrine of ideas has been dealt with above, pp. 28–29. The phraseology of the Platonic doctrine is echoed in Philo, not only in

---

[1] This imagery occurs in Plato *Rep.* 490 B; *Phaedr.* 256 E; *Symp.* 209 A–212 A. See Adam's note to *Rep.* 490 B, in his *Republic of Plato*, II, 15.

[2] Cf. also *Charmides* 155 E and see Aristotle *Pol.* 1287 a 30.

contexts where the ideas themselves are dealt with, but, by a kind of metaphor, in other contexts as well. The phrase ἀεὶ κατὰ ταὐτὰ καὶ ὡσαύτως ἔχει, which in Plato[1] expresses the stability and permanence of the ideas, is used by Philo, coupled with its equivalent ἄτρεπτον for permanence generally. Repentance has no share in the ἀτρέπτου καὶ ἀμεταβλήτου καὶ ἀεὶ κατὰ ταὐτὰ καὶ ὡσαύτως ἐχούσης φύσεως (De praem. 15). The κόσμος is described as ἀεὶ κατὰ τὰ αὐτὰ καὶ ὡσαύτως ἔχων in Somn. 2:220.

The word ἀποβλέπων or ἀφορῶν is frequent in Plato in connection with the ideas.[2] It occurs in Philo in similar contexts. See ἀποβλέπων εἰς τὸ παράδειγμα, in De op. mund. 18, 55; Conf. ling. 63; Quod Deus sit 108.

The figures by means of which Plato represents the relation between the idea and the particular color Philo's language in many passages.[3] Plato at times represents the idea as the original, of which the particular is the copy.[4] In Philo the Ten Commandments are described in language reminiscent of Plato's allegory of the cave, as ἀπεικονίσματα καὶ μιμήματα τῶν ἀγαλματοφορουμένων ἐν τῇ ψυχῇ παραδειγμάτων.[5] The vernal equinox is an ἀπεικόνισμα καὶ μίμημα of creation.[6] The eternal life of God is the παράδειγμα καὶ ἀρχέτυπος of time.[7] στάσις in the soul is the ἀρχέτυπος of all war.[8] In De post. C. 105, the perfect art is said to be a μίμημα καὶ ἀπεικόνισμα of nature. This passage is a reminiscence of Rep. 596 f. where μίμησις as a theory of art is connected with the theory of ideas. Philo goes on to say that the music of lyres and flutes is as far inferior to that of nightingales as ἀπεικόνισμα καὶ μίμημα ἀρχετύπου παραδείγματος, φθαρτὸν εἶδος ἀφθάρτου γένους. Such passages show how instinctive with Philo was the use of the Platonic phraseology.[9]

[1] Cf. Phaedo 78 C D E, 79 A; Rep. 479 A, 500 C; Symp. 211 B, et al.; Soph. 249 B. The phrase is used in Philo for the ideal world in De praem. 29; cf. also Leg. all. 3:99; Quis rer. div. 149; De plant. 49.

[2] Plato Crat. 389 A B;. Rep. 484 C D, 500 B-D, 501 B; Gorg. 503 E; Laws 625 E, 626 A, 630 C, 688 A B, 693 B, 707 D, 714 B, 743 C, 757 C, 770 C, 962 A D, 965 B, et passim.

[3] For an account of these figures see Adam, Republic of Plato, II, 172 f.

[4] Rep. 476 C, αὐτὸ . . . . ᾧ ἔοικεν; cf. Rep. 592 B, of the ideal city, ἐν οὐρανῷ . . . . παράδειγμα; also Rep. 596 B, 597 B.

[5] V.M. 2:11; cf. Rep. 514 E ff.   [7] Quod Deus sit 32.
[6] Sp. leg. 2:151.   [8] De post. C. 185.

[9] Cf. also De op. mund. 71; Mut. nom. 183; De praem. 29; Quis rer. div. 126, et al.; and cf. above, p. 52, n. 3.

8. OTHER PLATONIC FIGURES[1]

For other Platonic figures it will be sufficient to cite the passages. The list here given makes no claim to be exhaustive.

a) Nourishment of the soul:
  Plato: *Phaedr.* 247 D, 248 B, 246 D E; *Protag.* 313 C; *Phaedo* 84 B.
  Philo: *Fug. et Inv.* 137 f., 174; *Sp. leg.* 2:202; *Quis rer. div.* 79, 191; *De sac. A. et C.* 41; *Leg. all.* 1:98.

b) The "second voyage":
  Plato: *Phaedo* 99 C; *Pol.* 300 C; *Phil.* 19 C.
  Philo: *Somn.* 1:44, 180; *De Ab.* 123; *Decal.* 84.

c) Σκιαμαχία:
  Plato: *Laws* 830 C; *Rep.* 520 C; *Apol.* 18 D.
  Philo: *De cherub.* 81; *De plant.* 175; *Quod. det. pot.* 41.

d) War in the soul:
  Plato: *Phaedr.* 237 D; *Rep.* 439 C f., especially 440 B.
  Philo: *Quis rer. div.* 243–46, 284; *Cong.* 92, 175 f.; *Somn.* 1:174, 2:147, 284; *De gig.* 51; *Mig. Ab.* 56, 62; *De eb.* 75, 98, 104 f.; *De Ab.* 105, 223 f., 240; *De virt.* 184; *Leg. all.* 1:86, 2:91, 3:117, 130, 131, 134, 186.

e) The storm of life or of passion:
  Plato: *Rep.* 496 D, οἷον ἐν χειμῶνι-κονιορτοῦ καὶ ζάλης ὑπὸ πνεύματος φερομένου.
  Philo: *Conf. ling.* 32; *De sac. A. et C.* 16; *De post. C.* 22 f.; *Quod Deus sit* 26; *Cong.* 60, 93.

f) Unworthy wooers of Philosophy:
  Plato: *Rep.* 495 D E, cf. 489 D.
  Philo: *De eb.* 49–50.

g) Hitting the mark:
  Plato: *Theaet.* 179 C, οὐκ ἀπὸ σκοποῦ εἴρηκεν; cf. Homer *Od.* xi. 344, οὐ . . . . ἀπὸ σκοποῦ . . . . μυθεῖται βασίλεια.
  Philo: *V.M.* 2:2, where a quotation from Plato is introduced by φασὶ γάρ τινες οὐκ ἀπὸ σκοποῦ. The figure is developed and expanded in *De sac. A. et C.* 82; cf. *De sob.* 26; *Conf. ling.* 48, 103, 144; *V.M.* 2:151; *Quod det. pot.* 22, 65; *De op. mund.* 31, 41. For τοξότης applied to the Sophist cf. *Theaet.* 165 D, πελταστικὸς ἀνήρ used of the eristic questioner; Philo *Fug. et Inv.* 210; *De post. C.* 131.

---

[1] Cf. for the figure of the wax tablet pp. 62, 63, with n. 2; the figure of the sun, pp. 21, 59, n. 2, 65, n. 7; the figure of the seal, p. 52, n. 3; the figure of the baits of pleasure, p. 69, with n. 4.

h) The king as shepherd; reason as shepherd:
   Plato: *Rep.* 343 B.
   Philo: *De ag.* 50; *De Jos.* 3; *V.M.* 1:60–62; cf. *Quod det. pot.* 9, 25; *De sac. A. et C.* 48 f., 104; *De post. C.* 67.

i) Contrast between the cook and the physician:
   Plato: *Gorg.* 464 D ff.
   Philo: *De Jos.* 61–63; cf. *Quod det. pot.* 26.

j) Handing on the torch:
   Plato: *Laws* 776 B; *Rep.* 328 A.
   Philo: *Quis rer. div.* 37; *De op. mund.* 148; cf. *De eb.* 168, 212; *De gig.* 25.

k) Men as puppets:
   Plato: *Laws* 644 D E f.
   Philo: *Fug. et Inv.* 46; *De Ab.* 73.

l) Harmony of word and deed:
   Plato: *Laches* 188 D, 193 D E.
   Philo: *Frg.* (M., pp. 656, 663); *Fug. et Inv.* 150, 152; *Mut. nom.* 195; *De Jos.* 230; *V.M.* 1:29; 2:48, 130, 140; *Sp. leg.* 2:52, 4:134.

m) The body the garment of the soul:
   Plato: *Phaedo* 87 B–E.
   Philo: *Quaes. in Gen.* 1:53; cf. *De eb.* 101.

n) The body a prison:[1]
   Plato: *Phaedr.* 250 C; *Phaedo* 62 B, 67 D, 82 E, 114 B.
   Philo: *De eb.* 101; *Mig. Ab.* 9; *Quis rer. div.* 68, 85, 273; *Mut. nom.* 173; *Somn.* 1:139.

o) The scale:
   Plato: *Rep.* 550 E; *Tim.* 63 B.
   Philo: *De sac. A. et C.* 122; *De post. C.* 100; *De gig.* 28; *Quod Deus sit* 85; *Mig. Ab.* 148; *Fug. et Inv.* 151; *De Ab.* 196.

p) The drone:
   Plato: *Rep.* 564 B–E *et al.*
   Philo: *Mig. Ab.* 164.

q) The magnet:
   Plato: *Ion* 533 D E.
   Philo: *De praem.* 58; *De gig.* 44.

r) The body a tomb:
   Plato: *Gorg.* 493 A; *Crat.* 400 B C.
   Philo: *Sp. leg.* 4:188; cf. *Mig. Ab.* 16, 23; *Somn.* 1:139.

[1] Cf. supra, p. 69.

s) Planting:

Plato: *Phaedr.* 276 E, φυτεύῃ τε καὶ σπείρῃ μετ' ἐπιστήμης λόγους; cf. *Rep.* 492 A.

Philo: *Mut. nom.* 173, σπείρειν καὶ φυτεύειν τι τῶν κατὰ παιδείαν ἀδυνατοῦντα. This figure forms the basis of his interpretation of the garden of Eden. Cf. *De plant.* 32 ff., especially § 37.

9. PHILO'S USE OF OTHER STRIKING PLATONIC PASSAGES

This list, like the list of Platonic figures given above, makes no claim to be exhaustive. All that has been attempted is to illustrate Philo's dependence on the phraseology of his master.

a) Plato: *Phaedrus* 252 A, description of the man possessed by love—
μητέρων τε καὶ ἀδελφῶν καὶ ἑταίρων πάντων λέλησται καὶ οὐσίας δι' ἀμέλειαν ἀπολλυμένης παρ' οὐδὲν τίθεται.

Philo: *Sp. leg.* 1:52—"ἀπολελοιπότες" φησί, "πατρίδα καὶ φίλους καὶ συγγενεῖς δι' ἀρετὴν καὶ ὁσιότητα μὴ ἀμοιρείτωσαν ἑτέρων πόλεων καὶ οἰκείων καὶ φίλων."

De praem. 15—ζήλῳ δὲ καὶ ἔρωτι τοῦ βελτίονος ἐξαίφνης κατασχεθεῖσα καὶ σπεύδουσα καταλιπεῖν μὲν τὴν σύντροφον πλεονεξίαν καὶ ἀδικίαν.

De sac. A. et C. 129—οὗτοι καταλελοίπασι τέκνα, γονεῖς, ἀδελφούς, τὰ οἰκειότατα καὶ φίλτατα, ἵνα ἀντὶ θνητοῦ τὸν ἀθάνατον κλῆρον εὕρωνται . . . . τούτοις δὲ ὁ δρασμὸς ἑκούσιος δι' ἔρωτα τῶν ἀρίστων.

Fug. et Inv. 88 f.—καὶ γὰρ οἱ Λευῖται τρόπον τινὰ φυγάδες εἰσίν, ἕνεκα ἀρεσκείας θεοῦ γονεῖς καὶ τέκνα καὶ ἀδελφοὺς καὶ πᾶσαν τὴν θνητὴν συγγένειαν ἀπολελοιπότες. . . . . ἡ δ' ἀψευδὴς φυγὴ στέρησις τῶν οἰκειοτάτων καὶ φιλτάτων ἐστίν. This passage is also colored by φυγὴ δὲ ὁμοίωσις θεῷ, *Theaet.* 176 B, quoted in *Fug. et Inv.* 63.

Leg. all. 2:85—καὶ γὰρ ἐγὼ πολλάκις καταλιπὼν μὲν ἀνθρώπους συγγενεῖς καὶ φίλους καὶ πατρίδα.

De vit. cont. 13—τὸν θνητὸν βίον ἀπολείπουσι.

b) Plato: *Laws* 854 C—τῶν κακῶν ξυνουσίας φεῦγε ἀμεταστρεπτί. The imitations in Philo are affected by φυγὴ δὲ ὁμοίωσις θεῷ, *Theaet.* 176 B, quoted explicitly in *Fug. et Inv.* 63.

Philo: *De sob.* 13—κἂν ὅλην Αἴγυπτον ἀμεταστρεπτὶ φεύγων ᾤχετο.

Leg. all. 3:14—οὐ φεύγει . . . . ἀνεπιστρεπτὶ γὰρ ἂν ἀπεδίδρασκεν, ἀλλ' ἀναχωρεῖ.

Quis rer. div. 305—ἀποδρασόμεθα ἀμεταστρεπτί.

INFLUENCE OF PLATO ON PHRASEOLOGY OF PHILO 103

De virt. 181—πάγκαλον γὰρ καὶ σύμφερον αὐτομολεῖν ἀμεταστρεπτὶ πρὸς ἀρετὴν κακίαν.

De praem. 117—ἀμεταστρεπτὶ φεύγειν διεγνωκότα φυγήν, οὐ τὴν ἐπονείδιστον λεγομένην, ἀλλὰ τὴν σωτήριον. Compare *De eb.* 145, λιποτακτῆσαι τὰ θνητά.

c) Plato: *Rep.* ix. 571 D–572 A, the passage called by Pater in *Plato and Platonism*, p. 123, Plato's evening prayer. Note, in the Platonic passage, τὸ ἐπιθυμητικὸν .... μὴ παρέχῃ θόρυβον τῷ βελτίστῳ χαῖρον ἢ λυπούμενον, ἀλλ' ἐᾷ αὐτὸ καθ' αὑτὸ μόνον καθαρὸν σκοπεῖν .... τὸ θυμοειδὲς πραΰνας .... τὸ τρίτον δὲ κινήσας ἐν ᾧ τὸ φρονεῖν ἐγγίγνεται .... οἶσθ' ὅτι τῆς τ' ἀληθείας ἐν τῷ τοιούτῳ μάλιστα ἅπτεται.

Philo: *De vit. cont.* 27 f.—δυομένου (ἡλίου) δὲ ὑπὲρ τοῦ τὴν ψυχὴν τοῦ τῶν αἰσθήσεων καὶ αἰσθητῶν ὄχλου παντελῶς ἐπικουφισθεῖσαν, ἐν τῷ ἑαυτῆς συνεδρίῳ καὶ βουλευτηρίῳ γενομένην, ἀλήθειαν ἰχνηλατεῖν.

Sp. leg. 1:298—καθεύδοντες .... τῆς δὲ ψυχῆς ἐπικουφιζομένης τὰς φροντίδας καὶ ἀναχωρούσης εἰς ἑαυτὴν ἀπὸ τοῦ τῶν αἰσθήσεων ὄχλου καὶ θορύβου καὶ δυναμένης τότε γοῦν ἰδιάζειν καὶ ἐνομιλεῖν ἑαυτῇ. Cf. further *Somn.* 1:43.

d) Miscellaneous parallels:[1]

Phaedr. 243 D: ποτίμῳ λόγῳ. Cf. *Leg. all.* 2:32, ποτίμοις ἐννοίαις; *Sp. leg.* 2:62 and *Quod omnis prob. lib.* 13, ποτίμων λόγων.

Laws 631 C: πλοῦτος, οὐ τυφλὸς ἀλλ' ὀξὺ βλέπων. Cf. *De praem.* 54, πρὸ τοῦ τυφλοῦ τὸν βλέποντα πλοῦτον. Cf. further *Sp. leg.* 2:23; *Fug. et Inv.* 19; *De vit. cont.* 13.

Phaedr. 253 B: οἱ δὲ Ἀπόλλωνός τε καὶ ἑκάστου τῶν θεῶν οὕτω κατὰ τὸν θεὸν ἰόντες. Cf. *De vit. cont.* 12; *Sp. leg.* 1:20.

Laws 838 E: τοῦ μὲν ἄρρενος ἀπεχομένους .... μηδ' εἰς πέτρας τε καὶ λίθους σπείροντας κ. τ. λ. Cf. *De vit. cont.* 62.

Tim. 29 A: ὁ μὲν γὰρ κάλλιστος τῶν γεγονότων, ὁ δ' ἄριστος τῶν αἰτίων. Cf. *De praem.* 1, ὁ μὲν γὰρ ἀφθάρτων τελειότατος, ὁ δὲ θνητῶν φέρτατος (see Shorey, note in *Class. Phil.*, VII, 248); *De op. mund.* 82.

---
[1] See also above, p. 83, n. 7.

INDEX

1. ENGLISH

Allegorical method, 10, 66 ff.
Allixius, 4.
Ambrosius, 3.
Angels, 28, 43.
Aristotle, 22, 23, 31, 48 ff., 53 f., 60 ff.

Being, 16, 17, 18.

Chrysippus, 77.
Clement, 2.
Conscience, 84 f.

Demons, 42 f., 45.
Determinism, 70 f.
Dionysius Petavius, 4.
Dualism, 13.

Eclecticism of style, 10 f., 21 f.
Encyclic studies, 9, 86.
Eros, 17, 40 f., 68, 83 ff.
Eusebius, 1 ff.
Evil, 23, 70.

Fabricius, 5.
Flux, 23.
Freedom, 71.

God (see Table of Contents); determined, 18, 19, 20, 21; as Father, 19, 22; immanent, 19; controlling men, 75 f.
Grace, salvation by, 83.

Ideas, doctrine of, 76.
Idea of Good, 16, 21, 30, 79, 85.
Inconsistencies in Philo, 14, 18, 39, 45 f., 68, 71.

Jerome, 2.
Jewish elements in Philo, 11, 14.
Jewish opinions of Philo, 3, 8.
Jonsius, 5.
Justin Martyr, 3.

Le Clerc, 5.
Lipsius, 5.
Logos, law of the universe, 38; High Priest, 40; first-born Son of God, 39.

Materialism, opposition to, 13, 53 f., 55 ff
Mosheim, 6 f.
Mystic conceptions, 23, 58, 68.

Peripatetic doctrines in Philo, 76 ff.
Philosophy, 86.
Plato, rationalistic and mystic aspects, 11, 26; dualism, 13; theology, 14, 16, 17, 20 f.; Idea of Good, 16, 21, 30, 79, 85; doctrine of matter, 24; psychology, 47, 49, 52, 59 f., 63 f.; use of myth and allegorical interpretation, 66; doctrine of divine inspiration, 68; determinism and free will, 71; Philo differing from, 82; doctrine of salvation by grace, 83.
Pleasure, 68 f., 80 f.
Political virtue, 78 ff.
Posidonius, 8 ff., 44.
Punishment, 71, 87.

Stoicism, its teaching regarding the Logos, 30 ff., 34, 43, 44, 47; psychology, 49, 62; doctrine of moral progress, 81, 87; language of, used by Philo, 15, 22, 25, 53, 57, 71, 77, 87.

Theodore the Metochite, 3 f.
Transition, suggested by a phrase in the Platonic context, 89 f.

Virtues as means, 77, 78.

World, 23.
World-soul, 16.

2. GREEK WORDS OF ESPECIAL IMPORTANCE

ἕξις, 50.
πίστις, 72 ff.
πνεῦμα, 54 ff., 63.
τόνος, 57.
τῦφος, 73 ff.
φύσις, 50.
ψυχή, 50 f.

ANCIENT PHILOSOPHY

1. Otto Apelt. *Platonis Sophista. Recensuit, Prolegomenis et Commentariis Instruxit*
2. Grace Hadley Billings. *The Art of Transition in Plato*
3. Thomas H. Billings. *The Platonism of Philo Judaeus*
4. Ingram Bywater. *Aristotle on the Art of Poetry. A Revised Text with Critical Introduction and Commentary.*
5. Lewis Campbell. *The Theaetetus of Plato. A Revised Text and English Notes.* Second Edition
6. Henri Carteron. *La notion de force dans le système d'Aristote*
7. Harold Cherniss. *The Riddle of the Early Academy*
8. Ingemar Düring. *Aristotle's De Partibus Animalium. Critical and Literary Commentaries*
9. Ingemar Düring. *Aristotle's Chemical Treatise. Meterologica, Book IV. With an introduction and commentary*
10. Ingemar Düring. *Die Harmonienlehre des Klaudios Ptolemaios* bound with Ingemar Düring. *Porphyrios Kommentar zur Harmonienlehre des Ptolemaios*
11. Ingemar Düring. *Ptolemaios und Porphyrios über die Musik*
12. Wilmer Cave France. *The Emperor Julian's Relation to the New Sophistic and Neo-Platonism: with a study of his style*
13. John Gibb and William Montgomery. *The Confessions of Augustine.* Second Edition

14. Carlo Giussani. *T. Lucreti Cari De Rerum Natura Libri Sex. Revisione del testo, commento e studi introduttivi*
15. Sir Thomas Heath. *Mathematics in Aristotle*
16. William A. Heidel. *Selected Papers*. Edited with an introduction by Leonardo Tarán
17. Roger Miller Jones. *The Platonism of Plutarch and Selected Papers*. Edited with an introduction by Leonardo Tarán
18. Hal Koch. *Pronoia und Paideusis. Studien über Origenes und sein Verhältnis zum Platonismus*
19. Clara Elizabeth Millerd. *On the Interpretation of Empedocles*
20. Constantin Ritter. *Bibliographies on Plato* ("Berichte . . . über Platon erschienenen Arbeiten")
21. Léon Robin. *Pyrrhon et le scepticisme grec*
22. Richard Robinson. *Plato's Earlier Dialectic*. Second Edition
23. W.D. Ross. *Aristotle's Prior and Posterior Analytics. A Revised Text with Introduction and Commentary*
24. Paul Shorey. *Selected Papers*. Edited with an introduction by Leonardo Tarán
25. Paul Shorey. *The Unity of Plato's Thought*
26. G. Stallbaum. *Platonis Opera Omnia*. (This set is published here in fourteen volumes and includes Stallbaum's commentary on Plato's *Parmenides*.)
27. E. Seymer Thompson. *The Meno of Plato, edited with Introduction, Notes, and Excursuses*
28. Eliza Gregory Wilkins. *"Know Thyself" in Greek and Latin Literature*
29. John Cook Wilson. *On the Interpretation of Plato's Timaeus. Critical studies with reference to a recent edition*
    bound with
    John Cook Wilson. *"On the Platonist Doctrine of the ἀσύμβλητοι ἀριθμοί"*